T0368381

Also by the Author

"Good Bye, Mr Patel" 1st edition 2009

2nd edition 2010 Revised

Gentle Breeze of Daily Wisdom 2013

"Good Bye, Mr Patel" II The Sequel 2018

The Attributes of a
VIRTUOUS MINDSET

*Unveil Your Beneficence
and Magnificence
Embrace the Expansive
Landscapes of Higher
Consciousness*

ANIL KUMAR

authorHOUSE

AuthorHouse™ UK
1663 Liberty Drive
Bloomington, IN 47403 USA
www.authorhouse.co.uk
Phone: UK TFN: 0800 0148641 (Toll Free inside the UK)
*   UK Local: (02) 0369 56322 (+44 20 3695 6322 from outside the UK)*

Published by AuthorHouse 11/26/2024

ISBN: 979-8-8230-9107-7 (sc)
ISBN: 979-8-8230-9108-4 (e)

Library of Congress Control Number: 2024925166

Print information available on the last page.

This book is printed on acid-free paper.

Contents

About the Author

Anil Kumar, a retired chartered accountant, has spent 15 months crafting his latest work, *The Attributes of a Virtuous Mindset*. For Kumar, writing is more than expression—it is a spiritual practice, refining his thoughts and articulating his beliefs. His fourth book explores the transformative power of a virtuous mind grounded in values and inner purity. Divided into three segments—*Being*, *Doing*, and *Becoming*—it offers readers a path to self-realization and spiritual growth through upright thinking and courageous action.

A passionate writer, Kumar connects with a global audience through insightful quotes, blogs, and articles on existential topics. Beyond writing, he is an avid golfer and former cricketer, having represented East & Central Africa in the 1986/87 ICC Trophy. At 77, he mentors and occasionally delivers motivational talks.

Residing in Horley, Surrey, UK, with his wife Urmila, a retired nurse, Kumar cherishes family life. Together, they enjoy the company of their two sons, Nickesh and Russikesh, their wives and six grandchildren. Kumar dedicates this book to his late mother, Shardaben Patel, acknowledging her values and teachings as the foundation of the principles in his work.

Foreword

Exploring the Bounds of Human Understanding

The human mind is confined to conceptualisation, meaning 'whatever it can imagine exists within the bounds of its understanding' - an inherent limitation. As these concepts take form, they undergo a transformative process known as manifestation.

However, the mind struggles with its innate limitation; it cannot conceive of that which exists before the very notion of existence itself. Paradoxically, this constrained mind tirelessly seeks the origin of creation. It endeavours to unravel the mysteries of the Universe, tracing its inception from the monumental Big Bang and seeking to grasp its continuous expansion. This scientific inquiry, abundant in facts, encounters a profound question - **the state preceding the Big Bang** remains elusive, beyond the cognitive grasp of the mind.

Could it be that Nature has intentionally imposed this limitation? Despite extensive exploration and explanation, the continuum preceding what is already understood stretches infinitely. The human vocabulary lacks suitable replacements for terms like 'beginning' or 'origin,' and as the mind continues its quest, time constraints remain dominant, hindering it from transcending temporal boundaries. Is there perhaps an inherent purpose behind this limitation?

The inquiry deepens. Perhaps the very concept of what precedes, entangled in the fabric of time and space, eludes explication by the human mind. Is it conceivable that the mind must relinquish its confines, allowing the energy of the human spirit to propel it beyond the state of mere humanity?

Might it be that the solution to this inscrutable puzzle lies not in explanation but in experiential revelation? A revelation that dawns when humanity collectively senses its intrinsic oneness, merging with the entirety of the Universe. In this unity, a profound wonder unfolds - a state of total Integrity where time, space, and judgment dissolve. This transcendental state defies linguistic expression, rendering the mind obsolete in a realm where language holds no sway.

In the realm of this transcendental state, the culmination of experiential revelation unfolds as 'Mukti' - a liberation where the mind and ego gracefully release their grasp on the self. However, the prerequisites for this profound liberation demand a transformative evolution of the mind, achieved through unwavering commitment to diverse disciplines.

This transformative journey is intricately mapped across three foundational segments: **Being, Doing, and Becoming.** Each of these segments stands as a pivotal chapter in the narrative of personal growth and unfoldment. "The Attributes of a Virtuous Mindset" is an illuminating guide through this transformative odyssey, shedding light on the path toward self-realization and self-discovery. It ventures into the ethereal realm of mystical revelations, providing a beacon for those seeking to **transcend the** limitations of the mind and embrace the expansive landscapes of higher consciousness.

In the realm of 'Being', the book delves into the essence of self-awareness and mindfulness, exploring the core principles that lay the foundation for a virtuous mindset. Here, the book unravels the intricacies of understanding oneself, embracing authenticity, and portraying a deep connection with the inner self. As we navigate through the terrain of 'Being,' readers are invited to reflect upon their values, beliefs, working creeds and the intricate interplay of thoughts that shape their perception of the world.

The second segment, 'Doing', transcends the theoretical and steps into the realm of practical application. It explores the tangible actions and behaviours that manifest a virtuous mindset in daily life. From acts of kindness and empathy to ethical decision-making, this section is a practical guide to integrating virtuous principles into one's actions. 'Doing' is not just about performing deeds but cultivating a conscious and intentional approach to living, where **every action expresses a virtuous mindset.**

Delving into the profound realms of 'Becoming', this third segment delves more into the esoteric dimensions of the virtuous mindset - an exploration into the intricate tapestry of self-discovery and growth. Within this transformative sphere, readers are not only urged but initiated into the art of embracing change, triumphing over challenges, and seamlessly adapting to the perpetual ebb and flow of the personal development landscape.

'Becoming' emerges as an alchemical crucible, wherein the dynamic essence of the journey unfolds. It beckons individuals to recognise that self-realisation is not a static endpoint but an ongoing, perpetual process. In this metamorphic space, each experience is a thread intricately woven into the fabric of our evolving identity - a tapestry that expands with every nuance of growth and revelation. Here, 'Becoming' transcends mere evolution; it becomes a sacred passage, inviting readers to participate actively in the alchemy of self-discovery and, in doing so, to **unlock the esoteric depths of their Becoming.**

This contextualises our understanding of Nature's construct and workings.

Consequently, the paramount importance of unravelling the authentic truth about our collective existence renders our ceaseless preoccupation with nationality, race, religion, political affiliations, and daily conflicts for rights and privileges as utterly futile and self-imposed limitations. **There is much more to unravel about ourselves on this Planet.**

Beyond the boundless canvas of Nature's colourful creation, the resplendent paintbrush, the vibrant hues, and the multi-dimensional masterpiece **must lie the Creator – the Superintelligent Absolute.** To catch a glimpse of this mastermind, one might need to transcend the painting, entering a state of **mindlessness that unveils the secrets concealed within.**

In this limitless realm, there is an abundance for the mind to engage in and be exhilarated by, transcending the constraints of conventional thought and embracing the boundless possibilities that await exploration.

As we explore the attributes of a virtuous mindset, let us open our minds to the possibilities of transformation, challenge our preconceptions, and embark on a quest towards a more meaningful and purposeful existence. "The Attributes of a

Virtuous Mindset" beckons, promising not only insights into the facets of **Being, Doing, and Becoming** but also a roadmap to cultivating a mindset that ascends above the ordinary - **a state that leads to a life of profound fulfilment and purpose.**

THE BEING PHASE

Existence is not in the doing, but in the being that precedes it.

1st Virtue

BE INTEGRATED

To bring elements of love, care, respect, momentousness, and inner
spirit to bear on all one's words and actions is sincerity,
the cornerstone of integrity.

You and I

In all sincerity, as I begin this work, I am placing **You,** the
Reader, in the forefront of my conscious mind. You are the
spur that triggers me to pour out to You what is coming to me
from the force of inspiration. This force will keep us connected
during Your journey through this work.

To begin with, this is a monologue but intermittently
through the book, it will turn into a quasi-dialogue between
You and me because I want You to be immersed in what You
read, so much that You subconsciously put me at the centre of
the attendant chatter in your mind. The reading will bring a
natural flow of subliminal messages to You. If you must know,
a subliminal message is a series of imperceptible impulses sent
to someone's mind below the threshold of awareness. Equally,
your reactive expressions, opinions, or emotions, relating to

1

what You read in the book, will reach me assuming You direct thoughts to me.

There is nothing mysterious or spooky about this marvel of nature that is at work routinely in all humans but mostly without our awareness; we are less inclined to explore and get to know this curious natural phenomenon mainly through weariness and inertia. Seemingly it is our characteristic indolence that is preventing many of us from wanting to be inquisitive about the various miraculous powers and sensitivities in us; for example, experiencing events in the physical that echo prior thoughts or spoken words, and déjà vu which is an uncanny feeling of having lived through the present situation sometime in the past.

The New Year Frenzy

Be that as it may, at the stroke of midnight on 1 January 2024, the entire humanity was united in a hysteric frenzy amid a spectacular display of fireworks to draw a line between 2023 and 2024 to put the past behind us. You ushered in the new year with an exuberant cheer, hugged everyone in sight, and wished them a *'Happy New Year'*.

Just then my awestruck mind leapt back to 2022 and wondered: if an idea like a date can spur humanity to come together, why can't a nobler idea of resolve to draw a permanent line between war and peace put the unsavoury past behind us for good? Had only 1% of good wishes greeted by everyone that year come true, the world would not be in such a dire state now, more than one year later.

Were the wishes not sincere? Were they hollow and meaningless? Why does a new-year wish for good health, happiness, and prosperity not manifest any noticeable outcome? Is wishing anyone happiness, good health, or prosperity on an important occasion a vain effort? Is it done just to routinely conform to social norms such as shaking hands, hugging, kissing, or giving flowers? The answer is mainly an emphatic **Yes**.

What we say amounts to pseudo-words creating only a fleeting warmth and pleasantness. **We have become consummate practitioners of fakery** – the makers of nothing - burgers.

Power of words

Then what about the one major endowment gifted to mankind - the innate ability to speak and convey meaning through words? We live and breathe words. Words may be spoken or written, or unsaid and unwritten. Any which way they may be conveyed, they are potent seeds sprinkled from the mind or heart. A response will spring from them sooner or later.

"What we speak becomes the house we live in" - Hafiz

Words are the bricks and stones of the pillars of literature and the history of civilizations and nations. They may bear magical predictive ingredients. Legendary seers have brought iconic truths to mankind through words infused with prescience, and the vigour of prayer or a spiritual ritual is amplified by the repetitive enunciation of words and sounds.

Words are virtual connective tissues or hormones that arouse emotions of joy or despair.

Words sung by a mother to her unborn child will entrain the mother and child for life. No matter how far apart in life the two may be, their words when sung will close the space between them.

Even when uttered in silence, words can bring the world together just as they can set it apart. They change the most unbending of minds and hearts. Words are energy-propelling ripples in the air – the manifesters of thoughts into things. Depending on how they are spoken, the words create vibrations that even affect positively or negatively the growth of plants in your garden and summerhouse.

Powerful words when heard with clarity ring echoes in the mind of the listener and create lasting meaning. They may be sung or spoken, but when conveyed unseen and unheard amid the night, they are sublime influencers that build bridges between humans.

Such is the power of words that needs to be understood and embraced by humans as a tool with the potency to heal, comfort, encourage, arouse, or even demoralize others.

Heal your words to heal your wounds.

In practical life, do people follow up on the wishful messages they habitually send to others to find out how the recipients have been affected? The answer is mainly an emphatic **No** because it is not done in practice. These are perfunctory age-old obligatory protocols and rituals performed in any organized society. What people say in speech could be innocuous ringtones of polite gestures because that is what people do at the onset of a new year.

Sincerity

Truthfully, humans engage in all this disingenuous paraphernalia unthinkingly which may be viewed as harmless socializing, but the sobering truth is that it is a grave abuse, disregard for, and neglect of **sincerity – a highly esteemed character quality of candour and purity** that is vital for the effectiveness in any personal endeavour and interactions with others. **It is a wellspring of all other virtues and values for mankind to grow and groom.**

Sincerity is the precursor of budding trust for any relationship with others, including the Divine. **It is the mother of all trust.** It demands purity of mind and freedom from any ulterior motive, hypocrisy or any kind of falsehood. To be unrelenting in the dogged pursuit of any purpose is sincerity. The primacy of sincerity is one's natural inclination to bring elements of love, care, respect, momentousness, and inner spirit to bear on all one's words and actions. Most of all, sincerity is being conscionably steadfast in living by and applying one's resolutions, beliefs, and principles in all matters of life. To discern in a person deeply embedded sincerity demands a cognitively penetrative 'rock of eye' to visually get a true measure of a person's characterization.

Thought, emotion, word and action in harmony = Integrity

A sincere person with honest intentions is trustworthy. Anyone will readily open their door to such a being. Sincerity is a compelling quality of a trustworthy character that fittingly stands on the plinth of integrity – **wholeness,** the emulsified and fully aligned walk and talk, even behind closed doors. **Integrity is the spectrum at either end of which stand sincerity and trust.**

Honesty, truthfulness, and good intent are assimilated into this spectrum.

Where there is integrity, there is the perpetual existence of body, mind, and spirit in cohesion.

Our Unmaking

Unfortunately, in the modern highly materialistic social order, the universal existence of integrity is seen as a far-fetched utopian notion. Most of us gauge anyone's success by their measurable accumulations. To be more successful than others is seen as the greatest attainment which further attracts a higher status that becomes an exploitable conduit for more attainments in an indifferent world run by syndications, nepotism, favouritism, and selfish preferential treatment for reaping abundant rewards. The habitual lure of easy rewards leads to a widespread compromise of any principle-driven practices of integrity in financial or commercial matters.

Amid this droopy culture, to bring the inclination of the inner spirit to bear on all one's words and actions is an onerous act of integrity that can jeopardise all one's chances of attainment. In a nutshell, no one cherishes the idea of being integrous if it is to cost them a lucrative opportunity or avoidable taxes. **The ways of a society devoid of even a sliver of integrity are ephemeral and can only last a single season.**

When integrity wanes, reigns are given to pretence, apathy, deceit, hypocrisy, falsehood, and inauthenticity; there is less trust in all human interactions, and life shrinks proportionate to the dispiritedness of the mind. Even New Year's resolutions fail because they are devoid of any sustainable energy thrust of sincerity.

'My word is my bond' – the memory and practice of this idiom to express honourable intentions have faded. The spoken word ceases to matter and there is no shame or moral sense of failure when a debt or obligation is not fulfilled. The sense of trust is undermined putting strain on all relationships and modalities of social behaviour. Laws, rules, legislation, constitutions, charters, statutes, etc. of any empowered body or sovereign nation carry less weight because of the erosion of integrity on the part of those in authority.

The continued erosion of personal standards of integrity is leading to our unmaking. We fall apart at the seams when we entirely lose our mores – the basic sense of social right and wrong.

Already there is increasing disharmony in every walk of life. We are letting relationships fade into discord, but whilst the degenerating life can be endured with fortitude, what is essential for an idyllic social order is an ingrained understanding that at the deepest level all our actions, little and large, positive and negative, constructive and destructive, create subtle energetic waves that subsequently gather mass and momentum to either propel our social boat forward or rock it. Ultimately, only we are responsible for how the boat is sailing because we are the captains who set the sail. **If the captains believe our social boat is unsinkable even with our fast-eroding values and beastly ways, they are mistaken to the level of titanic proportions.**

A Paragon of Virtues

Live for the greater good of all

Life need not be as gloomy and gruelling as we may make it out to be. We should see no need to be dissatisfied with it or be shocked by the actions of politicians, businesses, others, or even natural forces, - let us not lash out in anger and frustration, but opt instead to be forgiving of everyone and every act we think has caused us pain. Life is pretty as it is – needing no fancy clothes or lipstick. It is the greatest gift of Creation. It simply needs a change in our perspective of it to hone our thoughts and behaviour. Perhaps simple childlike innocent, sincere, and ingenuous purity of uninhibited speech and unfettered action lived from the heart would create a social order of wholesome lives.

Amid all the misery You could think about **living life as if it were a book for Your grandchildren to read**. It will behove any individual to live as if society does not owe them a living and to cherish the ideal of self-reliance and pride in living with integrity and holding their head high such that when their grandchildren think of integrity, **they will think of them as a 24-carat paragon of virtues of excellence in all walks of life.**

I was only ten when my father died but his spirit comes alive when I am told how he endured, with dignity and great fortitude, the vicissitudes of life during the economic depression of the nineteen thirties and survived. I can only strive to be a paragon of virtues for my grandchildren so they may learn to live their lives from the heart rather than the deviousness of the mind so they may see their joys not in service to themselves but in their devotion to the well-being of the social environment for the greater good of all.

The Holy Trinity

To be integrated means bringing the body, mind, and spirit together to be one congruous whole like the Cosmos that is without discord. It is simply a case of striving to create a miniature cosmic world within.

A solemn commitment to integrity in all circumstances will keep You in tune with the Universe. Now you may turn cartwheels of joy and go forth knowing You are fully turbo-charged.

Auto-suggest to Yourself:

I am a born caring, compassionate, and authentic soul.
I strive to inculcate in me the attributes of the Cosmos.
I have emblazoned on the whiteboard of my mind a
sincere wish for integrated humanity, that I am a part of.

'**Be integrated**' is the 1st Virtue that makes You one within yourself ready to expand your horizons to live as if You are one with the Cosmos in eternal connectedness. This connectedness is also a profound experience of embracing a tender closeness with every fundamental element of existence and fostering an intimate unity with the Force responsible for All Creation.

In a state of integrity, You are an indivisible One, unyielding and unbreakable.

2nd Virtue

BE BEYOND FRAGMENTATION

There is a whole new world
hiding beyond the face of the illusory familiar.

If you eliminate the things that make you look at life fragmentarily,
your mind is then not following the rut. Therefore, it is free.
If you want to see the view of the valley from the hill, you survey the
whole thing, don't you?
That means your mind is no longer merely fixed on a particular part;
you look at the whole valley.
- J Krishnamurthi

Fragmentation refers to the ultimate disconnection between outer actions and inner selves. Seeing beyond fragmentation requires a shift in mindset - a transcendence of fragmented thinking to adopt a holistic perspective on life, relationships, and society. This shift is facilitated by practical methods like mindfulness, compassion, and embracing diversity and inclusivity in our daily interactions. By doing so, we pave the way for an inspired, harmonious, and interconnected worldview. For instance, consider the microcosm of a mother with multiple children who perceives them all as part of one cohesive family unit, illustrating the power of unified perception despite diversity. My late mother, widowed at 39, held the entire family of seven of us bonded together as one cohesive unit that prevails today as a blissful larger family of 54, sixty-seven years later.

Transcending fragmentation brings about an awareness of the interconnectedness of all aspects of existence and cultivates an understanding of holism. This expanded perception moves beyond isolated parts to offer a deeper comprehension of life and its complexities. At the core of reality lies an unbroken truth that fragmented thinking fails to fully grasp. By nurturing a truly creative imagination, unencumbered by doubt and cynicism, we can overcome these limitations and recognize the inherent futility of fragmentation.

The adoption of holism requires a curious mind that seeks an all-inclusive understanding of the world, rather than simply arriving at quick conclusions based on superficial observations. Seeing beyond fragmentation requires a willingness to explore the unknown and retrain the mind to be objective in its analysis and interpretation of new insights. By applying these insights to improve human behaviour, we can gain wisdom and work towards creating a better life for all. But before diving deeper into these concepts, it's important to address some questions you may have in your mind.

Q: What do you mean by fragmentation?

Very broadly, simply, and fundamentally, the failure to recognize the presence of your Maker within you, thus seeing yourself as singular and separate from the very source of all creation, is fragmentation - the very root of all suffering. I have in mind spiritual fragmentation, which refers to a state where someone feels disconnected from their inner self or the divine. It can manifest as a feeling of emptiness, a lack of purpose, or a sense of disconnection from one's higher self. In general, fragmentation refers to various aspects of human behaviour in society that go against the laws and tendencies of Nature, which are eternal, synergistic, comprehensive, stable, robust, caring, and dependable. Therefore, fragmented thinking leads to a life of disconnection, brokenness, confusion, chaos, and conflict, with a mind that lacks fluidity and flow. Acting as though 'the **self is supremely important and the perceived virtue in the performance of any act for the greater good of all is a myth'** are both indicative of a fragmented mind.

Similarly, failing to grasp the holistic concept that matter and energy are interconnected reflects a narrow perspective rooted in fragmentation. Such a mindset also struggles to comprehend the wisdom conveyed in the Upanishads, such as the notion that *"All that you see doesn't exist,"* because it remains confined to surface-level understanding and fails to delve deeper into profound truths.

This mind concludes that it has seen the whole valley without going to the top of the mountain.

Q: Then why see beyond fragmentation instead of fixing it?

If your mind is hopelessly stuck in a condition, you cannot effectively deal with it. To improve any condition, it is necessary to understand it properly, which is best achieved by taking a step back and viewing it from a different perspective. It can result in recognizing that you cannot fix the world, but you can fix yourself. Once you achieve internal integration, you naturally progress toward seeing life beyond fragmentation. This is a step towards achieving an integrated state with external conditions. Seeing beyond fragmentation is not a physical act but a transcendence or evolution of the conscious mind to a higher reality and a shift in perception.

This involves being consciously at one with every aspect of your life and accepting it completely nonchalantly. A conflict-free state protects your inner spirit and trains it to distinguish fact from fiction as new paradigms emerge from progressive transcendence. This is how the mind begins to repair the broken and fragmented world, by simply changing the way it perceives and experiences it. The phrase **"To kill the evil in a killer is preferable to killing the killer"** exemplifies the new clarity and shift in belief that occurs in the mind seeking a comprehensive solution to a problem.

Q: What are the consequences of living in fragmentation?

The way you react and respond to the world around you, which is your everyday environment, can have both positive and negative consequences that determine your future psychological and spiritual growth and happiness. But living in fragmentation can have negative consequences on your overall well-being and sense of wholeness. When you are fragmented, your thoughts, emotions, and behaviours can become disjointed, causing feelings of being disconnected from yourself and others. **This** can lead to feelings of anxiety, depression, and a lack of purpose or meaning in life. Your repeated experiences shape who you are. **If you live in a spiritually devoid and violent environment, you are likely to be negatively influenced by it.** This influence creates a society of self-centred individuals who lack the depth of understanding and seek quick fixes to contend with life. Such a society is characterized by insincerity, duplicity, selfishness, and short-termism.

On a positive front, it becomes clear that fragmentation is a product of the mind that drives behaviour. Eventually, you become disillusioned with your world and begin to see past the daily chaos. Your mind begins to extend itself beyond this chaos. The most significant outcome of this is that you begin to grasp the futility of your life. **You start to understand that many things and events in your daily life serve no real purpose.**

When you firmly grasp the abstractness of life, you begin to see dimensions that were previously unseen. You are in a new dawn, and you have a clearer sense of awareness of your body, mind, and spirit, which need to function as interconnected parts of one whole. This is holism within you, the antithesis of fragmentation, and the start of an evolutionary process to view your world from a new perspective. It becomes clear that there is less wonder and intrigue in what is seen, observable, and measurable in the world around you, rather than in what is hidden or unseen such as spiritual or supernatural phenomena in which you seek spiritual or supernatural experiences for comfort, guidance, or connection to something greater than yourself.

Ultimately, your innate senses strike upon new dashes of realism about life, and you begin to know that human thinking needs to be reprogrammed. You now understand the meaning of the phrase 'your world,' which refers to your daily interactions with people and events that directly affect You. 'Your world' does not include events like the war in Ukraine, the earthquake in Syria, the drought in Africa, or starving children in poor countries. These are realities beyond your direct influence, and you only know that they can impact your life economically and socially, but not spiritually. You have the wisdom, strength, maturity, and courage to live with these outside conditions while showing compassion and concern.

Q: Explain holism.

Let me share the words of Chief Seattle who was a Native American leader of the Suquamish and Duwamish tribes in the Pacific Northwest region of the United States in the 19th century. Here is what this wise leader said,

> **"Man did not weave the web of life, he is merely a strand in it.**
> **Whatever he does to the web, he does to himself.**
> **All things are bound together.**
> **All things connect"**

These words exemplify a deeper understanding of the interconnectedness of all things and the importance of recognizing our place within the larger web of life. They also highlight the idea that our actions have consequences not only for ourselves but also for the world around us. In the realm of philosophy and spirituality, holism refers to the perspective that sees all things as interconnected and interdependent, rather than isolated.

Matter and Spirit may be at the extreme ends of the
spectrum of cosmic setting
but ultimately, they are twin elements of existence.
The only difference is that matter is spirit
in slow motion, so as to be seen.

Holism is a way of understanding and embracing the diversity
of human societies, their customs, traditions, and systems. The
essence of holism can be illustrated by a musical orchestra or
choir, where the group functions as a unified whole in complete
harmony and synchrony. Any member of the group who is
out of sync with the others disrupts the entire performance,
signifying the importance of cohesion and interdependence in
achieving a common goal.

In a nutshell, Holism is the primal Oneness.

Q: Can Fragmentation and Holism co-exist?

No. The two cannot co-exist as they are two opposing mindsets.
Fragmentation arises from a distorted perspective and results
in a scattered, divisive, and chaotic approach to life. It sees
things as separate, isolated components without any recognition
of their interconnectedness or interdependence. It leads to
negative human traits such as selfishness, intolerance, violence,
and greed. On the other hand, holism is a way of thinking that
recognizes the interrelatedness of all things and emphasizes the
importance of the whole. It seeks to see beyond fragmentation and
embrace a state of oneness where there is no separation between
individuals or components. Holistic thinking is characterized
by an overarching view of the whole before making judgments

about individual parts. It is driven by the principle that each part of the whole is intimately interconnected and cannot have a meaningful existence independent of the other parts. In essence, holism prevents one from regressing into fragmentation and provides a framework for understanding and living with the diversity of human societies and their customs, traditions, and systems. **It is a mindset for creating unity, harmony, and integrity, rather than division and chaos. Expanding the heart, mind and horizons**

There are several reasons why there is a need to see beyond fragmentation, but most importantly to challenge our conditioning and assumptions, and expand personal growth and understanding of life for inner peace and greater happiness. By seeing beyond fragmentation, we can understand how different parts of a system or situation are dependent on one another. This can help us visualize the bigger picture and make more informed decisions. We can develop empathy for others and understand their experiences and perspectives. This can help to reduce conflict and promote cooperation which is of utmost need in the world today. Fragmentation leads to isolation and disconnection.

When we see beyond fragmentation, we can identify new patterns and connections for solutions to problems that may not be apparent when we focus solely on individual parts. Great, iconic, and enlightened individuals possess the ability to not just perceive but also reside mentally and emotionally beyond fragmentation. It is their secret to achieving a well-rounded persona.

The hallmarks of a seer beyond fragmentation.

A seer beyond fragmentation typically exhibits several hallmarks such as sensing and distinguishing dimensions that ordinary eyes fail to even see. Their senses are expanded beyond the ordinary level. They possess a mindset that understands and acknowledges the world as a unified entity. They view the human race as a collective whole, rather than disparate populations functioning as independent entities. This fundamental quality serves as a guiding principle for their major life decisions. They are so open-minded and receptive to new ideas and perspectives that they are willing to challenge their own beliefs and assumptions. They possess empathy and concern for others and can see beyond self-interest. They are a personification of wisdom, possess a deep understanding of life and its complexities, and are widely trusted to apply their knowledge and experience for sound decisions and judgments. Their creative heightened imagination and ability to think outside the box allow them to develop innovative solutions to problems. They live constantly in a state of gratitude with a sense of appreciation for the beauty and wonder of life and freely express gratitude for the people and experiences that enrich their lives.

Notwithstanding all the estimable qualities, they maintain a sense of modesty and humility, recognizing that their understanding of the world is limited and that there is always more to learn and discover.

Seeing and Understanding Fragmentation
and Holism in Practical Settings

By embracing a holistic mindset and recognizing the interdependence of all things, we can make more informed decisions that positively impact our lives and the world around us. Understanding the concepts of fragmentation and holism in practical life facilitates a deeper appreciation of the interconnectedness of things. For example, in a conventional setting, a doctor will examine a patient's illness and provide suitable medication based on official guidelines and standard practices.

However, in a holistic approach, the doctor will seek to understand the patient's psychological, physiological, and sociological states, which can result in an accurate diagnosis and a long-term effective remedy. In the context of environmental issues, a fragmented approach may focus only on reducing individual carbon footprints, whereas a holistic approach would look at the systemic issues of pollution and climate change and work toward **collaborative and collective solutions.**

In personal relationships, a fragmented approach may rank individual needs over the needs of the partnership, whereas a holistic approach would value the interconnectedness and interdependence of both individuals and work toward mutual growth and fulfilment.

Similarly, gender balancing and meritocracy in the workplace are crucial for the holistic development of an organization in which primarily all individuals embrace the philosophy, values, and principles of holism. Under holism, gender balancing and meritocracy can blend in a way that allows for a more integrated and equitable workplace. Holism emphasizes the **interconnectedness and interdependence of all aspects of life**, including gender and merit. This means that gender balance and meritocracy are not viewed as separate or competing values, but rather as complementary and necessary components of a healthy and thriving workplace.

Holistic approaches recognize that gender diversity is essential for a wellfunctioning workplace, as it allows for a broader range of perspectives and experiences. At the same time, meritocracy is also crucial, as it ensures that individuals are hired, promoted, and rewarded based on their skills, abilities, and contributions rather than their gender. In a holistic workplace, gender balance and meritocracy work in tandem, with both values being rated highly and appreciated. This can lead to a more collaborative and supportive work environment, **where individuals feel valued and empowered regardless of their gender or background.** Additionally, a holistic approach can lead to a more effective workplace, as individuals with diverse perspectives and skills **are more likely to bring new and innovative ideas to the table.**

Marriage and Holism

Marriage represents holism as it unites two individuals of any race, culture, nationality, or gender in holy matrimony. However, how the wedding ceremony is conducted and celebrated only represents a fragment of the overall concept of marriage.

It is an example of the interplay between fragmentation and holism, where marriage as a whole embodies holism, while the style and glamour of its execution and celebration represent fragmentation. A marital or committed romantic relationship can serve as a powerful illustration of the concepts of holism and fragmentation.

Outdated as it may sound, this conceptual relationship begins with a total commitment of each partner to the other in the relationship. It acknowledges that **both partners are interconnected and part of a larger whole.** This involves considering the needs and desires of the relationship as a whole, rather than just focusing on individual needs. It includes valuing open and honest communication, mutual respect, and a willingness to work together to create a harmonious and fulfilling partnership.

A holistic approach to marriage also acknowledges the impact that external factors, such as family, work, and community, can have on the relationship, and strives to integrate these factors in a balanced and healthy way. Overall, holism in a marital relationship emphasizes the importance of building a strong, supportive, and loving partnership that benefits both partners and the relationship as a whole.

Marriage and Fragmentation

Fragmentation in a marital relationship can occur when the couple experiences a breakdown in communication and emotional disconnection. This can lead to a sense of isolation and a lack of understanding between partners, creating a fragmented relationship. Fragmentation may also arise due to conflicting values or goals, infidelity, or unresolved conflicts stemming from violent or coercive behaviour, which create emotional distance between partners. The lack of emotional intimacy and connection can cause distress and may lead to the breakdown of the relationship if not addressed.

Wealth can cause fragmentation in a marital or romantic relationship in several ways. Firstly, if one partner earns significantly more money than the other, it can create an imbalance of power and lead to feelings of resentment or insecurity. The wealthier partner may feel entitled to make important decisions without consulting their spouse or may exert more control over household finances, resulting in a sense of disempowerment for the other partner. Additionally, the pursuit of wealth can become all-consuming, leaving little time or energy for the relationship. The wealthier partner may prioritize their career or financial goals over spending time with their spouse or may adopt a materialistic lifestyle that does not align with their partner's values.

Finally, the pressure to maintain a certain standard of living can also cause stress and strain in a relationship. The couple may feel compelled to constantly work harder and earn more to sustain their lifestyle, leading to feelings of burnout or financial strain. This can result in arguments about money and priorities and create a sense of disconnect in the relationship.

Punishment and Forgiveness

People have different ways of dealing with wrongdoing, like punishing or forgiving. These two ideas are often treated as separate things instead of being connected. Punishment is meant to stop bad behaviour and make things right, while forgiveness is meant to let go of anger or hurt. This way of thinking can cause problems because it only focuses on punishing the person who did wrong and doesn't look at the reasons behind their actions. On the other hand, the idea of holism suggests that everything is connected, and when someone does something wrong, it affects more than just the person who was hurt. Forgiveness can help heal relationships and make things better for everyone involved, while punishment can be a way to make sure the harm caused by the wrongdoing is addressed and that it doesn't happen again. Humanism says that people are important and can make their own choices. However, punishment can make someone seem like they're not human, just a label or a set of actions. Forgiveness can make it seem like only the victim's feelings matter, ignoring the fact that both the victim and the person who did wrong have the ability to grow and change.

To promote a more holistic and humanistic approach to punishment and forgiveness, society needs to recognize the interconnectedness of all individuals and the complex social, cultural, and economic factors that contribute to wrongdoing. This involves moving beyond the dichotomy of punishment versus forgiveness and exploring more restorative and transformative approaches to justice that give importance to healing, accountability, and community building.

Religion and Fragmentation

The presence of fragmentation is a common theme in many religious faiths, where the focus is on defining and upholding specific beliefs and practices that distinguish one religion from another. This fragmentation is seen in the diversity of religious beliefs, rituals, and interpretations of sacred texts, which often leads to differences and conflicts among different religious communities.

One area where this fragmentation is particularly evident is in the concept of God. While many religions believe in the existence of a supreme being, the attributes and characteristics assigned to this God vary widely among different faiths.

For example, some religions believe in a God who is compassionate and forgiving, while others believe in a God who is judgmental and punitive and some believe in the non-existence of God. Similarly, the way that worship or rituals are performed, and the way that religious texts are interpreted can also vary widely among different religions.

This fragmentation can lead to a compromise of the concept of one God, as the focus shifts from the unity and oneness of the divine to the differences and conflicts among different religious traditions. Rather than recognizing the underlying unity and interconnectedness of all things, the emphasis is on defining and doggedly defending specific beliefs and practices that separate one religion from another.

However, it is important to note that not all religious traditions emphasise this fragmentation. Some spiritual and mystical traditions emphasize the unity of all things and recognize the underlying oneness of the divine. These traditions often stress the importance of transcending differences and recognizing the underlying unity that exists in all religious traditions.

To promote a more holistic and inclusive understanding of the divine, it is important to recognize the presence of fragmentation in different religious and non-religious traditions and work towards a greater understanding and appreciation of the diversity of these beliefs and practices. This involves recognizing the underlying unity that exists in all things and moving beyond the differences and conflicts that separate us, but for this to happen man must come out of the dug-out of intransigence he has become accustomed to living in.

Other causes of Fragmentation

Perhaps most alarmingly, fragmented thinking can contribute to a world where individuals or groups become divided along specific characteristics such as gender, culture, or nationality. This mindset gives rise to a polarized environment where different groups struggle to connect, resulting in misunderstandings, conflicts, and, in extreme cases, violence.

One manifestation of fragmented thinking is the imposition of rigid gender roles and expectations, which perpetuate a narrow binary understanding of gender. This framework leaves little room for variation and forces individuals to conform to strict norms, leading to a loss of respect and empathy between genders, as well as instances of discrimination, violence, and inequality.

Similarly, fragmented thinking can fuel a cultural divide, as individuals and groups promote their own culture while dismissing or rejecting others. This attitude can breed conflicts and cause indifference, hindering efforts for cultural exchange and understanding.

Additionally, fragmented thinking can fuel nationalist ideologies that emphasise differences between nations rather than their shared humanity and mutual interdependence. This can result in border closures, trade sanctions, and other forms of hostility that exacerbate deprivation and conflict, potentially leading to wars.

Education can help

To counteract the negative effects of fragmentation, it is crucial to integrate and advocate for comprehensive and inclusive educational curricula at the school level. This proactive approach aims to cultivate a deeper understanding of the world and life, laying the groundwork for a more harmonious, equitable, and just society. However, it's essential to acknowledge a caveat: Do not be so guileless as to think education and honesty belong in one box. As the saying goes,

"The one who has never been to school may steal from his neighbour's garden, but the one who has been to a university may steal the entire neighbourhood."

Therefore, while education is vital, it alone does not guarantee moral integrity. By exposing students to diverse perspectives, histories, and cultures from an early age, we can imbue them with values of empathy, interconnectedness, and collaboration. Effective education equips students with critical thinking skills to navigate complexities, empowering them to bridge divides and promote unity in our increasingly diverse global community.

Real and reality

Existing beyond fragmentation requires a deep understanding of one's perceptions of the world and the events that occur within it, as well as the conclusions and lessons derived from these experiences. It is about being fully aware of what is 'real' versus what is 'reality', to avoid being misled.

Real and reality are not interchangeable terms, as there are countless interpretations based on different perspectives. To truly grasp reality, we must arrive at a common understanding that allows for only one perspective to prevail. For example, you may view the chair you're sitting in as real because you can see and touch it. However, from a broader perspective, the chair is made of wood that was once a tree, which grew from an acorn that carried the potential to become a mighty oak. This ultimate truth about the chair is the reality that transcends the fragmented view of it as merely a piece of furniture. **By recognizing this interconnectedness and the wider context in which events occur, we can move beyond fragmentation and gain a more holistic understanding of the world.** This perspective can help us to better manage conflicts and challenges, and to make choices that align with our values and aspirations.

What is derived from an original form or formless state may be called the end product but it is a limited mind's misconstrued reality, an illusion, because the limited mind wants to conclude and finish the process of understanding without a deeper inquiry that needs intensive thought and reasoning.

Real and reality are two related but distinct concepts. The word "real" typically refers to things that exist objectively, independent of our subjective experience. On the other hand, "reality" refers to the totality of what exists, including both objective and subjective elements. To illustrate these concepts in a holistic context, consider the example of the ocean and wave to understand how fragmented thinking fails to see the bigger picture of holism and connectedness. Imagine an ocean with countless waves, each one separate and distinct from the other. These waves appear to be individual and separate entities, each with its unique characteristics and movements. However, when we look at the ocean as a whole, we realize that the waves are not separate, but rather a manifestation of the larger body of water.

In another metaphor, we may see individual trees, animals, and insects as "real" entities, each existing independently of one another. However, this view fails to capture the true reality of the forest, which is a complex and interconnected ecosystem. In reality, the forest comprises many interdependent elements, such as the soil, sunlight, and water that sustain the trees, the insects that pollinate the flowers, and the animals that feed on the plants and each other. Without any one of these elements, the forest as a whole would not exist.

Whilst on the topic of the forest here is another case of our warped and shallow observation skills. While driving through a forest you are forced to stop your car. You tell your children you've stopped because "deer are crossing the road", but your son who is an environmentalist reacts and says, "No, the deer are not crossing the road, it's the road that's crossing the forest!"

Another example of the difference between real and reality in a holistic context is the concept of love. We may see love as a subjective feeling or emotion, which is "real" in the sense that we can experience it first-hand. However, the reality of love goes beyond our subjective experience and encompasses the way that love affects our relationships, our communities, and the world at large. **In a holistic view, love is not just an individual feeling, but a force that connects us to the world around us.**

When we act with love, we create a ripple effect that can transform the reality of those around us. **The essence of love lies in giving, not in receiving.** Love is the very essence of life and the fuel that propels human beings to engage with the world and connect with others. It is a force that is unconditional and transcends the boundaries of time, space, and circumstances.

Love is not merely an emotion that is felt when it is reciprocated or returned; rather, it is an energy that is generated from within and shared with others without any expectations or conditions. When we love someone, we do so because we recognize their intrinsic worth and value as human beings, and we want to contribute to their happiness and well-being. We do not love them with the expectation that they will love us in return or that they will behave in a certain way toward us. **True love is not dependent on the actions or reactions of the other person but on our ability to love unconditionally.**

The idea that love does not have to be returned or reciprocated is based on the understanding that love is an internal state of being that is not dependent on external factors. **It is a choice that we make to extend ourselves beyond ourselves and connect with others in a meaningful way.** When we love without expecting anything in return, we free ourselves from the constraints of ego and attachment and open ourselves to the boundless possibilities of love.

In essence, the power of love lies in its ability to transcend the limitations of our fragmented selves and connect us to a greater whole. When we tap into this universal force, we experience a sense of oneness with all beings and a deep sense of purpose and meaning in life. Therefore, love is not something that needs to be returned or reciprocated; it is the very sap of life that flows through us and connects us to the world around us. **Love is not an event. It is a natural process in constancy.**

A virtuous mind aspires to uncover the ultimate truth that transcends surfacelevel differences arising from diverse perspectives. It delves deeper to grasp the underlying principles and universal laws governing the world and its inhabitants. Such a mindset rejects fragmented views of reality and strives to integrate diverse perspectives into a unified whole. For instance, while watching your favourite sport, you may experience joy when your team is winning, oblivious to your friend's sadness as they support the opposing team. However, when you go beyond this narrow perspective and appreciate the game's overall quality, you tap into a holistic state of mind, deriving joy from the entirety of the experience.

The role of spirituality

Spirituality seeks a deeper connection with oneself, others, and the universe, and often involves a search for meaning, purpose, and transcendence beyond the physical world through practices such as meditation, mindfulness, and gratitude, which can help individuals cultivate a sense of inner peace and resilience in the face of fragmentation and chaos. Additionally, spiritual communities can provide a sense of belonging and social support, which can help individuals steer through the challenges of living in a fragmented world. It is a powerful tool for individuals to cultivate a sense of wholeness and connectedness.

Drawing from spiritual and scientific wisdom, it is clear that whatever we focus our attention on receives energy from us. This energy can either result in the growth and development of the observed object or its state, or it can sustain its current state. This powerful phenomenon of observation is akin to the power of words, which was discussed in the previous chapter. However, the impact of observation is even more profound, as it highlights the interconnectedness between ourselves and the environment around us.

There is no better illustration of connectedness than in an ancient Hasidic Jewish saying; **"When you walk across the field with your mind pure and holy, then from all the stones, and all growing things and all animals, the sparks of their soul come out and cling to you, and then they are purified and become a holy fire in you".** It is crucial to recognize and embrace this wisdom cherished by the ancients that we are inherently wired to influence our surroundings. The energy we emit through our thoughts, emotions, and actions can have a significant impact on the world around us. Therefore, we must approach our environment with mindfulness and intentionality, recognizing the power we hold to shape the world around us.

By focusing our attention on positive, life-affirming qualities and actions, we can create a ripple effect of positive change that extends beyond our immediate surroundings. Conversely, when we dwell on negative thoughts or engage in destructive behaviours, we contribute to a cycle of negativity and suffering in the world.

Ultimately, the power of observation and thought highlights

the immense responsibility we hold as individuals to shape the world around us.

By embracing our interconnectedness with the environment, we can cultivate a greater sense of purpose and meaning in our lives, as we work towards creating a more harmonious and compassionate world for all beings.

Finally, here is a total encapsulation of the central theme of this Virtue:

What is here, is there, is everywhere. When you bond with these words you will know holism which is inseparability, the futility of going to war with your neighbour.

To truly experience and feel connectedness with All, be of a mind that is pure and holy, go to the seaside and dare to take a handful of warm beach sand. Now hold it in the open palm of your hand and let the tip of your nose sense familiarity with our forebears in the aroma of the sand. Your vibrant heart has just honoured and greeted your ancestry and caressed your destiny.

Now you know eternal connectedness and the ultimate pointlessness of fragmentation.

3rd Virtue

BE YOUR HIGHER SELF

It believes in its inner essence.
So, the forlorn pitiful seed grows into a mighty oak,

'**Your Higher Self**' is your idealized version that symbolizes your highest values, aspirations, and potential. Once awakened and integrated within yourself, and connected holistically with your outer surroundings, it is a certainty that you will fully discover and develop your inner strengths and attributes for more effectiveness and fulfilment.

The idea of striving to become our best selves has been a fundamental aspect of all humans for centuries. From ancient philosophical traditions to modern selfhelp movements, the pursuit of self-improvement has always been an integral part of our personal and spiritual growth. One of the most important ways we can achieve this is by tapping into the part of our inner self that gives abode to our ideals and aspirations - the cathedral of our "higher self," Our highest ideals and aspirations reflect our deepest beliefs, noblest intentions, and loftiest goals.

They include spiritual awareness and all natural sense virtues. Unlike learned virtues, which are acquired through education or socialization, natural sense virtues are believed to be part of our instinctual human nature. They are the foundation for ethical conduct and moral decision-making, guiding individuals to act in ways that promote the well-being of themselves and others. They may also encompass our aspirations for personal growth, such as developing our talents, building strong relationships, contributing to society, or cultivating a sense of inner peace and harmony.

When we tap into these values and aspirations, we connect with a sense of purpose and direction that guides our actions and shapes our character. We become more mindful of our thoughts, feelings, and behaviours, and we strive to integrate them into our highest ideals. In doing so, we elevate ourselves to a higher level of consciousness and make a positive impact on the world around us. We live by our values; thus, we stand out and others turn to us for guidance and mentorship which facilitates a sense of contribution and fulfilment.

There is less need to make a deliberate effort after you have embraced the virtues of these qualities and assimilated them into your daily routine.

Here are some ways in which these qualities can be developed:

<u>Compassion:</u> Compassion is the ability to feel and express empathy for others, and to act in ways that alleviate their suffering. It can be developed by cultivating mindfulness, practising active listening, volunteering, and engaging in acts of kindness and service. At the sharp end of the spectrum of awareness is Mindfulness, a skill to be present and fully engaged in the current moment, without judgment or distraction. Judgment

ejects you out of the capsule of Now. Mindfulness involves paying attention to one's thoughts, feelings, and surroundings in a non-reactive way. This can lead to greater self-awareness, reduced stress and anxiety, and improved mental and physical health. Active listening is, first of all, a habit of respecting the speaker that involves fully focusing on, understanding, and responding to them. It involves giving enthusiastic attention, seeking clarification, and paraphrasing what you heard. It creates a deeper understanding and builds stronger relationships.

Wisdom: Wisdom is the application of knowledge and experience that promotes mature understanding, insight, and astute judgment. It can be developed by seeking out new information, learning from mentors and teachers, reflecting on past experiences, and practising critical thinking and **self-reflection**. Selfreflection means looking inward and examining one's thoughts, emotions, behaviours, and motivations. It involves introspection and self-awareness, as well as a willingness to be honest with oneself and identify areas for personal growth and improvement. Self-reflection can lead to greater self-understanding, enhanced decision-making, and improved relationships with others. It can be practised through various methods such as journaling, meditation, and seeking feedback from others.

Courage: Courage is the mental or moral strength to persevere or withstand adversity, challenges or fear, and to come to terms with the worst that can happen. Then the will to resolutely confront fear, adversity, or risk in pursuit of a goal comes naturally. It can be developed by stepping outside of the comfort zone, taking calculated risks, practising resilience, and standing up for what is right.

<u>Justice:</u> Justice is the belief in fairness, equality, and ethical behaviour. It can be developed by being educated about social justice issues, advocating for marginalized groups, and taking action to promote fairness and inclusion.

<u>Humility:</u> Humility is the quality of being modest, unassuming, and open to feedback and criticism. It can be developed by practising gratitude, acknowledging limitations, seeking out diverse perspectives, and embracing a growth mindset.

<u>Love:</u> Love is the capacity to feel and express deep affection and connection towards oneself, others, and the world around us. It can be developed by cultivating self-love, practising empathy and compassion, nurturing relationships, and experiencing the beauty of nature and art.

<u>Spiritual Awareness:</u> Spiritual awareness involves an understanding of connection to something greater than oneself and a sense of purpose and meaning in life. It can be developed by meditation or other contemplative practices, connecting with a community of like-minded individuals, and embracing the mysteries and wonders of life.

Examples of people who are known for being their higher selves may include spiritual leaders, humanitarians, social activists, artists, and most of all everyday individuals who lead a low-key life with integrity and a commitment to making the world a better place.

Below are a few examples of legendary fictional characters created by their authors or actual historical personalities that illustrate the qualities of individuals who lived or are living in accord with their highest selves. Although the fictional characters were conceived in the minds of their creators, it is worth noting that anything that the human mind imagines with intensity and purpose can become possible, and you may be able to see or desire to inculcate some of these qualities in yourself:

Jonathan Livingston Seagull is the central character of the novel by Richard Bach. He is a seagull who is different from his flock as he is obsessed with flying and exploring new limits. Jonathan believes that there is more to life than just the daily struggle for food and survival. He embarks on a journey of self-discovery, **pushing himself beyond his limits, and striving to be his higher self.** He spends countless hours practising his flying skills, breaking speed and altitude records, and learning new techniques to fly with grace and precision. As he progresses on his journey, Jonathan becomes increasingly isolated from his flock, who cannot understand his passion for flying. **He realizes that he must follow his path, even if it means being alone.** Ultimately, Jonathan achieves his goal of flying at the highest level of existence and **becomes a teacher** for other seagulls, **sharing his knowledge and experiences** with those who are willing to learn.

Jonathan Livingston Seagull is characterized by a strong sense of purpose, a willingness to push beyond normal limits, and a commitment to following his path, even if it means being in isolation.

Siddhartha is a novel written by Hermann Hesse that tells the story of a young man named Siddhartha who goes on a spiritual journey to find enlightenment. Siddhartha leaves his comfortable life as a Brahmin to seek answers to the fundamental questions of existence. Along the way, he encounters various spiritual teachers and experiences both pleasure and pain. However, he ultimately realizes that true enlightenment cannot be taught but must be experienced through individual self-discovery. Throughout the book, Siddhartha strives to be his higher self by pursuing his inner voice and seeking to understand the nature of existence. He learns the importance of **self-reflection, compassion, and detachment from material possessions.** Siddhartha's journey toward enlightenment shows that the path to self-discovery is not always easy, but it is ultimately rewarding for those who are willing to undertake it.

Malcolm X, in his autobiography, describes his journey from being a petty criminal to becoming a prominent **civil rights activist**. Throughout the book, he highlights his struggles with racism and his efforts to overcome them. Malcolm X's **transformation from a violent, angry young man to a more tempered, thoughtful leader** is a testament to his desire to become his higher self. He educated himself, embraced Islam, **questioned his beliefs, and worked towards creating a more equitable society.** He also stressed the importance of self-respect and self-love, encouraging others to **find their inner strength** and not accept the injustices of society.

Mahatma Gandhi, in his autobiography, My Experiments with Truth, reveals his inner struggles, ethical dilemmas, and the **evolution of his principles and beliefs.** Gandhi strove to be his higher self by practising and promoting the principles of **nonviolence, truthfulness, and compassion.** He believed that these principles were essential for personal and social transformation. Gandhi also lived a simple and austere lifestyle, and **his commitment to these principles was unwavering, even in the face of opposition and adversity.** Gandhi's autobiography reveals his journey toward **self-improvement** and his **quest for truth and spirituality.** Through his experiences and reflections, he provides insights into how one can strive to be their higher self by cultivating virtues and living in alignment with their values and principles.

Nelson Mandela, also known as Madiba, was a South African anti-apartheid revolutionary who fought for equality and justice for all. He spent 27 years in prison for his activism and was subjected to inhumane treatment, yet he emerged from imprisonment as a highly evolved individual who had the strength to forgive and the vision to unite a divided nation. During his imprisonment, Mandela practised self-reflection, read extensively and developed his spiritual and intellectual capacity. He was committed to the principles of non-violence and reconciliation, which he believed were essential for the healing and transformation of South Africa. He used his experiences of suffering and struggle to inspire others and lead the country toward a peaceful transition to democracy.

After his release from prison, Mandela continued to work toward reconciliation and became the first democratically elected president of South Africa. He established the Truth and Reconciliation Commission to investigate and address human rights violations during apartheid, and he worked to promote education, healthcare, and economic opportunities for all South Africans.

Mandela's dedication to justice, equality, and reconciliation made him a beloved and respected leader, not only in South Africa but throughout the world. His legacy continues to inspire individuals and movements that strive for social justice and peaceful coexistence.

The Dalai Lama is the spiritual leader of Tibet and an advocate for peace, compassion, and nonviolence. He believes that true happiness and inner peace come from cultivating a sense of inner contentment and treating others with kindness and respect. The Dalai Lama has dedicated his life to promoting human rights, religious harmony, and environmental conservation. He has written numerous books and given countless lectures on these topics, inspiring millions around the world to live more fulfilling and meaningful lives. Despite facing persecution and exile from his homeland, the Dalai Lama remains committed to his mission of spreading compassion and understanding to all people.

Dr Martin Luther King Jr. was an American Baptist minister and civil rights activist who became one of the most significant figures in the American Civil Rights Movement. He believed in nonviolent resistance and civil disobedience to bring about change, inspired by the teachings of Mahatma Gandhi and his Christian beliefs. Dr King was a gifted orator and delivered some of the most memorable speeches in American history, including his famous "I Have a Dream" speech. He fought against racial segregation, poverty, and war, and his work led to significant changes in U.S. law and society. Dr King was also a Nobel Peace Prize laureate, receiving the award in 1964 for his efforts in combating racial inequality through nonviolent resistance. Sadly, he was assassinated in 1968, but his legacy continues to inspire people around the world to work toward social justice and equality.

Mr Spock, a fictional character in the Star Trek TV series, is a half-human, half Vulcan with traits such as pointed ears, enhanced strength, and agility. He is known especially for logical and rational thought processes and dazzling problem-solving capabilities. He stands out for his adherence to the principles of Vulcan philosophy, which emphazises reason and the suppression of emotion. Despite his stoic exterior, Spock is a deeply compassionate and moral character who is committed to the well-being of his crewmates. He often serves as a voice of reason and ethical guidance for Captain Kirk and the rest of the crew and is known for his unwavering commitment to upholding Starfleet's principles of peace, cooperation, and exploration. Spock's character embodies many virtuous attributes, including a commitment to reason and logic, a deep sense of compassion and morality, and a dedication to serving a greater purpose. **His character has become a cultural icon** and continues to inspire fans around the world.

St. Padre Pio was an Italian Catholic priest who lived from 1887 to 1968. He was known for his piety, his painful experiences with stigmata, and his jovial nature. Stigmata are the wounds of Christ that appear on a person's body, and Padre Pio experienced them for most of his life. He had wounds on his hands, feet, and sides that bled profusely and caused him immense pain.

Despite his suffering, Padre Pio was known for his sense of humour and his ability to connect with people. He had a gift for healing, and many people came to him seeking his help. He would pray with them and sometimes offer them a piece of his clothing as a token of his blessings. Padre Pio's healing miracles are welldocumented, and many people believe that he had the power to cure even the most serious illnesses. He was also known for his ability to read people's souls and give them guidance and advice, apart from appearing in two places at once.

Today, Padre Pio is venerated as a saint by the Catholic Church, and his shrine in San Giovanni Rotondo, Italy, attracts millions of visitors each year. His legacy lives on through the many people who have been touched by his teachings, his healing miracles, and his compassionate nature.

Jidhu Krishnamurthy, 1895 – 1986, was an Indian philosopher and speaker who spent his life promoting the idea of "total freedom" from conditioned thinking, beliefs, and prejudices. He believed that organized religion, rituals, and superstitious beliefs were all examples of conditioned thinking that prevented individuals from experiencing true freedom and fulfilment. He emphasized the importance of self-awareness, introspection, and questioning one's own beliefs and assumptions. He believed that true education should aim to develop a person's intelligence, creativity, and sensitivity rather than just imparting knowledge and skills.

Throughout his life, Krishnamurthy gave countless talks and wrote many books, sharing his ideas on human consciousness, spirituality, and personal transformation. He inspired many people around the world and his talks and writings continue to influence the world of philosophy and spirituality.

These souls and characters exemplify a vast array of virtuous values including compassion, wisdom, courage, justice, humility, love, spiritual awareness, and enlightenment. Their stories and accounts continue to inspire countless individuals to live in alignment with their higher selves.

Conclusion:

Being **Your Higher Self** means exemplifying virtues, values, and qualities of character that profoundly enrich your life and the lives of those around you. It entails staying rooted in your values while remaining open to flexibility, setting an example for others on their journey toward self-improvement, constantly evolving, and reflecting on your inner truth. Although it may not always garner the same attention or recognition as other pursuits, living as your higher self can inspire and influence others toward virtuous living.

Symbolically, you are like a soaring eagle, gliding effortlessly through life's currents, or a compass guiding others toward their inner truths and higher aspirations.

'Being Your Higher Self' is a pathway toward unfoldment and spiritual growth, rooted in the essence of who we are as individuals - our 'Silent Chant' within.

4th Virtue

BE YOUR SILENT CHANT

To be perpetually inspired and to live vibrantly, with all dormant forces enlivened, is to be your 'Silent Chant'.

As we progress on the journey of personal growth and spiritual fulfilment, we come to realize the significance of developing our mental and spiritual faculties. The preceding three virtues have laid a crucial foundation for this advancement, as we delve into the ideas of integrating the body, mind, and spirit, connecting with the external world, and attaining our higher selves. This chapter involves cultivating an awareness of our inherent divinity and embracing life with childlike ebullience.

Defining 'Silent Chant'

"Silent chant" is a metaphorical term representing the deepest essence of our individuality. 'Be Your Silent Chant' calls us to live effortlessly, immersed in eternal grace, fully connected to our inner essence and the mystical universe. In the words of Patanjali, it encourages us to *"let our thoughts break their bonds... let our mind transcend limitations and... discover ourselves to be greater persons by far than we ever dreamed."* It embodies a deep sense of security and gratitude for the gift of life, akin to the music inherent within us from birth, allowing for boundless creativity and wisdom.

Embracing this state, we manifest our ideas into reality, living with aplomb, confidence, composure, and freedom from stress. From these spiritual heights, we gain insight to predict and uplift others' lives, tapping into the mystical secrets of the universe. To embody one's "silent chant" is to reside in the purest essence of oneself, recognizing and embracing inherent mental and spiritual abilities that transcend the physical realm. These encompass abstract reasoning at the sharpest end, intuition, awareness of thoughts and emotions, and the capacity to express love and life. Through introspection and habitual self-reflection, we nurture and amplify these attributes, viewing them as manifestations of a divine source or the Creator.

The Construct of the "Silent Chant"

The concept of "silent chant" is given credence in many ancient religious and spiritual scriptures, as it is seen as a powerful means of connecting with the divine. The scriptures explain and provide different perspectives on the inner strengths and capabilities placed in humans. For instance, according to the Upanishads, a collection of ancient Hindu texts, dating back several thousand years, containing philosophical and spiritual teachings, each person is born with a unique set of talents and abilities that are part of their inherent nature. These talents are often hidden or obscured by various factors such as societal expectations, personal fears and doubts, and lack of guidance or mentorship. Furthermore, the Upanishads also emphasize that **these hidden talents are not just meant for personal gain, but are to be used for the benefit of others.** In other words, the realization of one's talents is seen as a path toward service and contribution to the greater good - beneficence. The Upanishads do not provide specific examples of hidden talents. However, they do emphasize the idea that each individual has a unique set of talents and abilities that are part of their inherent nature.

Some examples of these hidden talents could include artistic abilities such as painting, music, or dance; intellectual abilities such as problem-solving, critical thinking, or innovation; physical abilities such as athleticism or coordination; or social abilities such as empathy, communication, or leadership. However, the Upanishads suggest that these talents are not limited to these specific examples and that each individual has a unique combination of talents and abilities that are waiting to be discovered and developed. The Upanishads encourage individuals to look within themselves, reflect on their true nature, and seek guidance to uncover and develop these hidden talents.

This knowledge is crucial in fully embracing our "silent chant", the internalized component of our construct. **It encompasses our inclinations, preferences, fears, likes, and dislikes.** Our inclinations are tendencies towards certain behaviours or actions. For example, some people may be inclined towards creativity, while others may be inclined toward analytical thinking. These inclinations are shaped by our genetic makeup and environmental factors, such as upbringing and life experiences.

Our preferences are our choices or desires towards certain

things or experiences. For example, we may prefer a certain type of food, music, or lifestyle. These preferences are influenced by our tastes, cultural background, and individual experiences.

Our fears are the emotional responses to perceived threats or dangers. They are deeply rooted in our subconscious and can be triggered by various stimuli, such as social situations, phobias, or traumatic experiences. Our fears can limit our potential and prevent us from taking risks or pursuing our goals. Our likes and dislikes are our emotional responses to certain experiences or things. We may like certain foods, activities, or people while disliking others. These preferences are shaped by our tastes, values, and experiences.

Our construct is a complex and deeply ingrained aspect of our being, which influences our thoughts, emotions, and behaviour. It is unique to each individual and cannot be fully understood or shared with anyone else. However, through introspection and self-awareness, we can gain a deeper understanding of our construct and use it to live a more fulfilling and authentic life.

Our "silent chant" is deeply embedded in our subconscious. Through meditative exercises, we can alter it and harness agreeable thoughts while dismissing the rest. By intimately intertwining ourselves with our silent chant, we reach a state of total integrity and thus, we can become potent architects of our destiny. Others are drawn to us, and we can subliminally impart our cohesiveness and influence consciousness thus suggesting that it is possible to unconsciously convey a sense of unity to others, and by so doing, the collective mindset or awareness can be affected. In other words, people can subliminally communicate a sense of harmony and interconnectedness without necessarily being aware of it, and this communication can have an impact on the consciousness or the way people perceive and understand the world around them. This could happen through subtle cues such as body language, tone of voice, or shared experiences, which can create a sense of coherence and contribute to a shared understanding among individuals or groups.

The essence of the "silent chant" is not merely a phrase but a representation of our authentic selves - an ever-present, dynamic aspect that dwells within us, even if often unnoticed. This essence lies deep within, silent yet keenly attuned and responsive when we engage with it. It epitomizes our genuine nature, ingrained in every facet of our being, untouched by external factors like social status, career, or possessions. Instead, it links us to something beyond the material world. The notion of an aircraft "black box" can be metaphorically understood as the repository of our innermost essence or truth. Similar to how a black box records and preserves crucial flight data, our silent chant encapsulates our deepest thoughts, emotions, and spiritual essence.

When we commune with our silent chant we tap into a wellspring of inspiration, wisdom, and insight readily available to us. This inner resource aids us in decision-making, offers clarity on significant matters, and guides us through life's trials with greater ease and grace.

The essence of the silent chant resonated within **Dr Viktor Frankl** during his harrowing ordeal of torture and captivity. His unwavering connection to this inner truth sustained him through unimaginable suffering, serving as a beacon of resilience and hope in the darkest of times. Like Dr Frankl, we, too, can draw upon our silent chant as a source of self-trust, strength and guidance, enabling us to endure adversity with fortitude and find meaning even amidst life's greatest challenges.

The shades of "silent chant"

Each person's "silent chant" or authentic self is unique and individual and can manifest in different ways. Just as there are different shades of colour, there are different shades or variations of the silent chant that can be expressed through a person's thoughts, feelings, and actions. Some people may connect with it through meditation or prayer, while others may express it through inner resilience, art, music, sport, or writing. This line acknowledges that there is no one-size-fits-all approach to connecting with one's authentic self and that each person's journey to discovering their silent chant will be different.

Marcus Rashford is an English professional footballer who plays for Manchester United and the England national team. He has used his platform to advocate for social justice and to raise awareness of food poverty in the UK. Rashford's "silent chant" is his commitment to using his platform for good and his belief in the power of community to create positive change.

Being aware of the inner silent chant and the presence of the 'authentic self' can be immensely helpful in constructing a successful and blissful life. When we are aware of our silent chant, we become more attuned to our thoughts and beliefs. We become conscious of the patterns of our thinking and can begin to identify any negative or limiting beliefs that may be holding us back. By consciously directing our thoughts towards positive affirmations and mantras, we can reprogram our subconscious mind towards more positive and constructive patterns. This can help us build confidence, resilience, and a sense of purpose that are essential for success in any endeavour.

By connecting with our authentic selves, we tap into a deep well of wisdom and guidance that is always available to us to overcome challenges and navigate the ups and downs of life with greater ease and grace whilst staying focused in all circumstances.

With the awareness of our inner silent chant and the presence of our authentic self, we cultivate a deeper sense of self-awareness and inner stillness. This allows us to tune out distractions, noise, and negativity and focus on what truly matters in our lives.

We become more mindful of our actions and decisions and can make choices that are relevant to our values and aspirations. This can help us live a more purposeful, fulfilling, and blissful life, free from the constraints of external expectations and societal pressures.

However, connecting with our "silent chant" is not always easy. It requires us to be given to stillness and quiet, to listen to the inner whispers, and to be open to the guidance that comes from within. We must learn to quiet the noises of our external world and turn our attention inward, where we can access the wisdom and guidance that resides within us.

In brief, **the "silent chant" is the essence that resides within each of us**. It is our fundamental silent ally, always present and ready to listen whenever we commune with it. As soon as we recognize the existence of this inner source of energy, our

authentic self, we start to comprehend that we are never alone or helpless. Our silent chant is our calling.

The hallmarks of a person embracing and being their "silent chant"

It's important to recognize and utilize these inherent divine treasures, while also aligning our lives with these internal endowments. Living in harmony with these legacies embodies the essence of the "Silent Chant," which encompasses all of the divine gifts bestowed upon us. The term "silent chant" can be interpreted in different ways, but it generally refers to the idea of espousing certain principles or values through one's actions and behaviour, rather than explicit articulation through words or slogans. Here are some hallmarks personified by people who are known for being their "silent chant":

<u>Consistency</u>: A person who is living the silent chant is consistent in their behaviour and actions, regardless of the situation or context. They do not compromise their values or principles for personal gain or convenience. **Gandhi's** consistency was evident in his personal and political life. He lived a simple lifestyle and consistently adhered to his principles of nonviolence, even in the face of violence and oppression from those who opposed his ideas. He was a paragon of consistency for his commitment to social justice and equality, advocating for the rights of the poor, marginalized, and oppressed throughout his life.

<u>Authenticity</u>: They are true to themselves and do not pretend to be someone they are not. They live their lives in accord with

their innermost beliefs and values. **Frida Kahlo** was a Mexican artist who is best known for her self-portraits, which often depicted her physical and emotional pain.

She lived in the early 20th century and was a prominent figure in the Mexican art world. Kahlo's authenticity was evident in her personal and artistic life. She lived her life on her terms, refusing to conform to societal norms and expectations. She often dressed in traditional Mexican clothing and rejected Western beauty standards, embracing her unique appearance and style. In her art, Kahlo explored themes of pain, identity, and gender, often drawing from her own experiences and emotions. Her self-portraits were deeply personal and raw, revealing her physical and emotional struggles with illness, injury, and heartbreak. Despite facing numerous challenges in her life, including a debilitating bus accident that left her with lifelong physical pain, Kahlo remained true to herself and her artistic vision. Her authenticity and individuality continue to inspire artists and audiences around the world to embrace their own unique identities and experiences.

Humility: They are not boastful or arrogant about their actions or beliefs. They do not seek recognition or accolades for their attainments, but instead, they do what they believe is the right thing to do. **Nelson Mandela** was a South African anti-apartheid revolutionary, political leader, and philanthropist who served as the first black president of South Africa from 1994 to 1999. Despite his long imprisonment and subsequent rise to political power, Mandela remained humble and dedicated to serving his people. He is widely admired for his ability to forgive his oppressors and work toward reconciliation between different racial groups in South Africa. He recognized that no one person or group could bring about lasting change alone, and he worked tirelessly to build bridges between different communities and promote unity and understanding. Despite his immense popularity and influence, Mandela remained grounded and focused on the needs of others. He lived a modest lifestyle and was known for his willingness to listen to others, seek feedback, and learn from his mistakes. His humility and commitment to service were evident throughout his life, making him a beloved figure in South Africa and around the world.

Empathy: A person who lives by their silent chant is empathetic and compassionate toward others. They try to understand others' perspectives and treat them with kindness and respect. **Mother Teresa** was a Catholic nun and missionary who dedicated her life to serving the poor and sick in India. She founded the Missionaries of Charity, a religious congregation that provides charitable services to people in need around the world. Mother Teresa was known for her deep empathy and compassion toward others, particularly those who were marginalized or suffering.

She saw the face of Jesus in every person she met and believed that every individual deserved love and respect, regardless of their circumstances. Renowned for finding people in pieces and leaving them in peace, she lived a life of service, spending her days caring for the sick and dying in the slums of Calcutta. Her selfless dedication to others and her unwavering commitment to helping those in need earned her the respect and admiration of people around the world. Mother Teresa's empathy and compassion towards others have inspired countless individuals to follow in her footsteps and devote their lives to serving others. She is considered a symbol of love, kindness, and humanitarianism, and her legacy continues to inspire people around the world to this day.

<u>Courage:</u> They are not afraid to stand up for what they believe in, even in the face of opposition or adversity. They are willing to take risks and make sacrifices to uphold their values. **Rosa Parks** was an African-American civil rights activist who became known as the "Mother of the Modern Civil Rights Movement." In 1955, she refused to give up her seat on a Montgomery, Alabama bus to a white passenger, which was required by the laws of segregation at the time. Her arrest for this act of civil disobedience sparked the Montgomery Bus Boycott, a yearlong protest that led to the desegregation of the city's buses. Parks' refusal to give up her seat was an act of immense courage, as it was a direct challenge to the deeply ingrained racial prejudices and segregation laws of the time. Her defiance of the status quo inspired others to join the struggle for civil rights and helped to ignite a national movement for racial equality. Despite facing threats and intimidation, Parks continued to fight for justice throughout her life. She worked alongside other civil rights leaders such as Martin Luther King Jr. and continued to speak out against discrimination and inequality until she died in 2005. Rosa Parks' courage and determination in the face of oppression and injustice have inspired countless individuals to stand up for what is right, even in the face of adversity. She is remembered as a symbol of the power of ordinary people to effect change and make a difference in the world.

Self-reflection: They constantly reflect on their actions to ensure they are aligned with their values. They are open to feedback and willing to learn from their mistakes. **Socrates** was a Greek philosopher who lived in Athens during the 5th century BCE. He is known for his method of questioning, known as the Socratic method, which was a way of exploring ideas and arriving at truth through dialogue and critical thinking. Socrates was committed to the idea that true knowledge could only be attained through self-reflection and examination.

He believed that individuals should constantly question their own beliefs and assumptions to arrive at a deeper understanding of the world and their place in it. Socrates famously declared that "the unexamined life is not worth living," and he dedicated his life to challenging the prevailing beliefs and opinions of his time through rational inquiry and self-reflection. Despite facing persecution and ultimately being sentenced to death for his ideas, Socrates remained steadfast in his commitment to the pursuit of knowledge and truth through self-examination. His legacy continues to inspire philosophers and thinkers to this day, and his emphasis on self-reflection as a means of personal growth and understanding remains as relevant as ever.

A person who is living their "silent chant" is deeply committed to their values and principles and demonstrates this commitment through their actions. For instance, **Jacinda Ardern,** the former Prime Minister of New Zealand is known for her compassionate and empathetic leadership style. She has been praised for her handling of the Christchurch Mosque shootings and her government's response to the COVID-19 pandemic. Ardern's leadership style and focus on social justice issues have had a significant impact on New Zealand. Her "silent chant" is her commitment to kindness and her belief in the importance of putting people first.

These legendary individuals lived or continue to live their 'silent chant' with an unwavering dedication to their values and vision, inspiring generations to come by expressing their values and principles in all aspects of their lives, even in the face of adversity. Their legacies continue to serve as a powerful reminder to us never to betray what truly matters to us in life.

The Credence for the concept of "Silent Chant"

Credence for the concept of the "Silent Chant" reverberates across major religions, underscoring the universal appeal of meditative practices and inner contemplations. In Christianity, the contemplative tradition, epitomized by the practice of prayer, emphasizes silent communion with the divine. Similarly, within Islam, Sufi mystics engage in silent dhikr, a form of recollection and meditation that goes beyond verbal expression. The Buddhist tradition, with its focus on mindfulness and meditation, echoes the essence of silent chant in cultivating inner awareness. Hinduism's ancient practices, such as Japa meditation, involve the silent repetition of sacred mantras, aligning with the concept of a silent chant.

These cross-cultural manifestations affirm the timeless credence in the transformative power of silent contemplations, offering a shared pathway towards spiritual connection and enlightenment.

Let your "Silent Chant" be a call to discover and harness the inner energy to connect with the mystical universe.

Your "Silent Chant", the inner truth, is your guide on your journey of deep selfdiscovery. Embrace it for within you lies the gateway to unravelling life's ineffable mysteries and wonders that weave through the cosmic complex of layers.

As you step into the **'Doing'** phase, remember that your 'Silent Chant' will be your steadfast companion, guiding you through the journey ahead. Embrace its wisdom and resonance as you advance towards the path of action, for therein lies the key to unlocking your fullest potential.

THE DOING PHASE

*Action is the brushstroke of purpose
upon the canvas of reality*

5th Virtue

AFFIRM AND EXUDE LIFE

To live deeply immersed in the essence of existence, to express reverence for life and appreciate the Creator for bestowing it upon us is to affirm and exude life.

Life is a mysterious force that permeates every living thing, manifesting itself in a myriad of ways. It is a force that cannot be tamed but can be **affirmed and exuded with humility**. To affirm and exude life is to become a conduit for its infinite power, to radiate its light from within, and to align ourselves with the divine essence that enlivens all existence.

This essence, due to its vibratory nature, remains an enigma to the human mind. Science recognizes the sacred truth that every particle is underpinned by a highly intelligent force that induces its vibration. This force is an essential aspect of our existence, shaping us into miniature replicas of itself and determining our ability **to be, have, and create all that we desire**. Embracing this fact is fundamental to affirming and exuding a fulfilling life and expressing vitality through our silent chant.

The purpose of life is not to be confined to a definition but rather expressed as a voyage of self-exploration and the creation of one's reality through thoughts, beliefs, and actions. Its ultimate goal is to kindle a realization within individuals that they are spiritual beings, encouraging them to live in harmony with their core principles and aspirations. Recognizing that the spirit within oneself is identical to that of others instils a sense of reverence, prompting one to establish compassionate connections with others. Life means **'Living In Full Embrace'** such that we gracefully receive all aspects of life, both positive and negative, and live without holding back or fearing the unknown. It is a reminder to live with open hearts and minds, to be fully immersed in every experience, and to appreciate the beauty and blessings of life while also learning from the challenges and difficulties.

The Japanese term **'Uketamo'** encapsulates the essence of living with openness. It can be translated as "I accept with an open heart" or "I receive with an open heart." It conveys a sense of openness, receptivity, and willingness to accept something with sincerity and without resistance reflecting an attitude of embracing what comes, whether it be opportunities, challenges, or experiences, with a sense of openness and acceptance.

Affirming Life

The affirmation of life begins with a profound admiration and a sense of wonder toward the magnificent beauty of the creation that surrounds us, coupled with a desire to unravel the mysteries of nature's essence and mechanisms. It is akin to the eagerness and curiosity of a child attempting to reach the moon. As our consciousness expands, it paves the way for a genuine sense of purpose and meaning, enabling us to approach life and its circumstances with composure and mindfulness. The one who truly affirms life is set apart from the rest by their unique character and nature. Here are their main traits and attributes:

Mindfulness

Individuals who affirm life are distinguished by their quality of mindfulness, characterized by their ability to bring attention to the present moment with an open and non-judgmental mind. This detachment from all sensations allows them to perceive and respond to life events without becoming entangled in them, living mindfully even in everyday activities such as walking, eating, or interacting with others. With heightened self-awareness, individuals who practice mindfulness can regulate their emotions and improve their overall well-being and mental clarity. Mindfulness also enhances the perception and appreciation of life, while cultivating greater resilience to meet challenges and opportunities with ease. Those who fully integrate mindfulness into their being exhibit remarkable ease in dealing with recurring life events of all kinds. They regard life as consciousness in perpetual motion.

Kindest to the Hilt

Imagine yourself as a fountain of kindness, endlessly bubbling with compassion and empathy. Like a fountain, you overflow with generosity, quenching the thirst of those in need with your acts of kindness. Being kindest to the hilt means allowing this fountain of kindness to gush forth freely, enriching the lives of everyone it touches.

To be kind to the hilt is to live a life imbued with heartfelt empathy. Those who affirm life inherently possess kindness within them and embody the maxim, **'The fact that I care means a great deal to the other person.'**

They are committed to recognizing and honouring the worth and dignity of all beings, working towards creating a more loving and just world for everyone. Kindness is not merely a habit in their interactions with loved ones but extends to strangers and even perceived adversaries. They actively listen with an open heart and mind, offering empathy, understanding, and support whenever possible. Knowing that their kindness is not only therapeutic for others but also for themselves, they treat themselves with the same compassion and respect they show to others, including setting healthy boundaries and practising self-care. Performing a small act of kindness can bring about a positive impact on both the giver and receiver without causing any harm. They consummately let compassion flow as bliss in motion.

Allowing the divine light of kindness to radiate through oneself illuminates the world with optimism and empathy.

A Consummate Giver

Giving is a fundamental and primal action that is inherent, and to affirm life is to emulate the character of nature itself. Being a consummate giver refers to a person who is deeply committed to giving of themselves to others in a way that is generous, selfless, and genuine. This trait is often associated with individuals who have a strong sense of empathy, compassion, and a desire to make a constructive impact on the lives of others. They put the needs of others before their own and are attentive and receptive to the needs and wants of those around them. Being a consummate giver is not merely about giving material or tangible things; rather, it involves giving of oneself in a selfless and heartfelt way. This cuts across cultural, racial, gender, or any other boundaries, allowing for recognition and connection at the level of human emotions and feelings.

This culture of giving is so universal that it extends to even the most impoverished and marginalized individuals. For instance, a beggar may silently greet a wealthy person who overlooks and walks past them with the words, *'I am so blessed that I share these times with such prosperous and privileged beings.'* **This simple gesture reflects the beggar's innate understanding of unity with all beings and the power of gratitude in cultivating an abundant mindset.**

Embracing Connectedness

To affirm the value and sanctity of life in the most sacred way, one must embrace and live life as though deeply immersed or, rather, pickled in connectedness and devoted to the support of all living beings and their inherent beauty. This requires a shift in perspective, moving from a limited self-focus to a broader awareness of the symbiotic relationships between all living things and recognizing that our choices and actions have an effect not only on ourselves but also on the other life forms around us.

When we embrace and live life as if we are pickled in connectedness, we can see the beauty and diversity of the world around us and recognize our place within it. We can appreciate the interdependence of all living beings and understand that our well-being is innately tied to the well-being of others.

Living in connectedness also involves recognizing the responsibility that comes with our interconnectedness, which means being mindful of our actions and choices and making decisions that reflect a deep respect for ourselves, others, and the world around us.

In essence, living as if you are pickled in connectedness is a sacred expression of the affirmation of life. It is a commitment to living in a way that reflects this understanding.

The concept of connectedness suggests that all beings and things in existence are interconnected and interdependent. Therefore, any action taken by an individual towards any other entity in this web of life, whether it be a living being or the environment, ultimately affects the individual. If we harm another being or the environment, we are also harming ourselves because we are all connected and part of the same grand matrix of existence. Similarly, if we act with compassion and kindness towards others, we are also benefiting ourselves because of the coherence we create in the world.

Thus, the golden rule of treating others as you would like to be treated is not only a moral principle but also a practical one based on the interconnectedness of all things in the matrix of existence. The essence of the Universe is responsiveness.

It does not take a genius to figure out that events are not isolated incidents that happen independently of one another. Instead, events are connected and influenced by other events, people, and circumstances, forming a complex web of causality. The interconnectedness of events can also be seen in personal relationships, where a single action or word can have a significant effect on the emotions and behaviours of others. This can lead to a cascade of events that affect the dynamics of the relationship and the well-being of the individuals involved.

Connectedness is a fundamental aspect of life, manifesting in many forms such as our relationships with loved ones, our interconnectedness with all living beings, and the broader interconnectedness of events and experiences. Embracing these forms of connectedness can lead to a deeper sense of meaning and purpose in life, as well as greater empathy, compassion, and a sense of responsibility towards others and the world around us. It is therefore undeniable that a conflict in some distant land will have some kind of effect on your life.

Practising kindness, mindfulness, and being a consummate giver are all the means to cultivate and strengthen these connections, ultimately leading to harmony.

Affirming life is not merely a passive act but an active one that requires a conscious effort to engage with the world around you. It involves recognizing the inherent value and beauty of all life, including your own, and striving to enhance and preserve it. When you affirm life, you cultivate a sense of purpose and meaning that imbues your actions and interactions with vitality and energy. This sense of aliveness is infectious and spreads to those around you, spurring them to live more fully and passionately.

Here is a sample of personal statements that exemplify one's affirmation of life:

✞ I am capable of transcending my limitations.

✞ Life is a precious gift, and I am grateful for every moment.

✞ Every day is an opportunity to learn, grow, and become a better version of myself.

✞ I am here for a reason, and I am committed to fulfilling my purpose.

✞ Challenges are opportunities for growth and development.

✞ I am connected to all living beings, and I treat others with kindness and compassion.

✞ The world is full of beauty and wonder, and I choose to focus on the positive.

✞ I am responsible for my happiness and well-being, and I make choices that support my health and vitality.

✞ I am capable of achieving my goals and dreams, and I take action to make them a reality.

✞ Every day is a new beginning, and I embrace each moment with joy and enthusiasm.

✞ Life is a journey. I am grateful for the experiences, people, and lessons that I encounter along the way.

These affirmations, or others you choose, can serve as your foundational belief statements becoming deeply ingrained in your consciousness and manifesting in your character and actions.

Exuding Life

You are exuding life when your actions speak out loudly to the world *"I am here. Look at me!"*. It is an uninhibited expression of the fundamental nature of being which is to exist and to thrive. It involves embracing the present moment, nonjudgmentally accepting and appreciating yourself and others, and living in harmony with the universe. Exuding life is a form of self-actualisation, where you can tap into your full potential and express your unique essence to the world with a sense of joy, purpose, and fulfilment. As you exude life, you recognize the inherent worth and dignity of all beings and act in a way that promotes their liveliness and well-being. This is a display of compassion, kindness, and empathy, as well as virtues such as patience, gratitude, and humility. Like a candle, you not only illuminate the surroundings but also give warmth and comfort to others around you.

As you affirm life, you naturally begin to exude it, and LIFE (Living In Full Embrace) ceases to be a mere acronym, transforming into a commitment to living fully, radiating verve, gratitude, and joy in all that you do.

Exuding life entails embodying vibrant, energy-infused actions that not only transform you but also emanate outward, impacting the world around you. By nurturing a mindset of vitality, enthusiasm, and optimism, you can overcome obstacles and channel your energy towards positive outcomes with a fervent zest for life. By embracing and integrating these practices into daily life, individuals expand their consciousness, gaining deeper insights into life's mysteries.

Children can be a portrayal of how life is exuded. Unrestricted by the qualms of adulthood, they exude life through their natural sense of curiosity and wonder. Constantly exploring and learning about the world around them, they are not jaded by the experiences that can come with age. They have no inhibiting ego, fear of failure, rejection, or mockery. One of the ways children exude life is through their unfettered natural sense of playfulness. The clock on the wall is meaningless to them as their normal inclination is to be fully engaged in the moment, whether they are playing with toys, exploring their surroundings, or interacting with others. This sense of playfulness is often infectious and can spur others to let go of their inhibitions and enjoy the present moment. Children wear their emotions on their sleeves. They may laugh, cry, or express themselves in other ways that are unfiltered, prolific and genuine. They reveal God to the world.

It is not only children who exemplify this but also many adults. One of the finest examples of an adult exuding life is when Muhammad Ali lit the Olympic flame in the 1996 Atlanta Olympics despite his Parkinson's disease, inspiring countless people around the world with his enthusiasm, energy, and unwavering commitment to his values, charisma, and passion for life.

Tiger Woods exuded life through his incredible golf performances, as well as his resilience in overcoming personal and professional setbacks. He has shown a remarkable ability to bounce back from injury and personal turmoil, and his dedication to his sport and his drive to succeed have inspired many.

Nick Vujicic, an Australian motivational speaker, was born with a rare disorder characterized by the absence of all four limbs. Despite his physical limitations, he has inspired millions with his positive attitude, resilience, and determination. He travels the world sharing his message of hope and faith and has written several books on overcoming adversity and achieving success. His example shows that any person can exude life even in the face of significant challenges.

Kabir, a 15th-century Indian mystic poet and saint who was a weaver by profession remains an influential figure revered by both Hindus and Muslims. His teachings focused on the importance of unity, tolerance, and love that cross religious and social barriers, emphasising living a simple life and the power of devotion to God. His poetry often dealt with themes of love, devotion, and the quest for spiritual enlightenment. Kabir's message of unity and equality of all people regardless of their caste or religion made him a prominent figure in Indian spiritual and cultural history. His poetry and philosophy focused on the idea of the divine being present in all creation and emphasized the importance of a personal relationship with the divine rather than formal religious practices.

His message of universal brotherhood and oneness has influenced generations of spiritual seekers and continues to inspire people around the world today. Kabir himself never identified with any particular religion or caste, and his teachings emphasise the unity of all religions and the importance of personal experience over religious dogma. Kabir embodies and personifies the essence of an affirmed and exuded life and serves as the 'silent chant' in the lives of numerous enlightened individuals.

Overall, the concept of exuding life entails a holistic and integrated approach to life, where your physical, emotional, mental, and spiritual aspects are all aligned towards a common goal of living a fulfilling and meaningful existence. It is an exuberant expression of gratitude for the Revered Giver.

**To inhale the potency of your existence, to articulate
your beliefs and emotions,
to radiate your brilliance, and allow it
to beam forth from within you
is to affirm and exude life.**

6th Virtue

BE IN YOUR THOUGHTS

You are truly in your thoughts when your 'working creed'
makes a permanent home in your consciousness.
Then you will understand the use of thought force
and make of yourself what you will.

To **"be in your thoughts"** means to ask yourself "What is in my mind at this very moment?" and thus to have a high level of acute awareness of the content of your mind. This enables you to have control over your actions, behaviours, and ultimately your reality. Negative or unhelpful thoughts can be identified and replaced by constructive thoughts. Your thoughts are incredibly powerful and can shape the course of your life. You are truly alive when conscious of your thoughts – your inner treasures.

Take a mindful pause to observe the vibrant interplay of thoughts, emotions, and mental images unfolding within your awareness. Tune into the subtle sounds of your environment, perhaps the distant hum of traffic or the soft murmur of nearby conversations. Can you detect any nuanced sensations or discomfort in your body? Are you attuned to the fluctuations in temperature or the prevailing sense of stillness in the air? You will note amid this act of reading, your mind, consciously and unconsciously, steers through or participates in rolling swathes of experiences.

Functioning as the command centre of our being, the mind orchestrates a symphony of processes enabling consciousness, perception, thinking, judgment, and memory. Remarkably, it manages an intricate maze of tens of thousands of thoughts each day during waking hours alone. Serving as the hub for our thoughts, emotions, and behaviours, the mind is the conduit for engaging meaningfully with the world around us and building human experience.

The Source of Thought

Thoughts constitute the bedrock of human consciousness. Take comfort in the recognition that there is self-edifying enrichment in the pursuit of the source of thought. Investigating the origin of thoughts is not just a curious exploration of internal mechanisms. It is a flight into the awareness of external factors - experiences and the environment - that shape the inception of thoughts, and, in turn, drive actions and behaviour. While the intricacies of the internal thought generator involving neurons, connections, and the release of various chemicals remain enigmatic, acknowledging this gift of nature beholds an understanding that our mental and physical states are intricately woven from the fabric of thoughts – **we become our thoughts**.

Much like a minuscule seed's potential to burgeon into a mighty tree, a single thought possesses the transformative power to influence our lives significantly. When we entertain a thought, we create a mental image or representation, and this imagery holds the potential to materialize in diverse ways, contingent upon the thought's nature and the energy and intention fuelling it. Just as a seed can multiply, a single thought can spawn related thoughts and emotions in a chain reaction, showcasing the interconnected nature of our mental landscape. Despite the incessant inquisitiveness about the source of thought, personal research and inquiry, based on individual experiences, knowledge, and mental faculties become invaluable tools. Relying on personal beliefs and drawing insights from credible sources throughout history becomes a compass for navigating the realms of thought exploration.

Unveiling the Potency of Thought

In the expansive landscape of the human mind lies the formidable power of thought, an intangible force that shapes the reality we inhabit. Each thought, akin to a potent wave of energy, possesses the capacity to mould our experiences and influence the course of our lives. Serving as an instrument for unlocking our complete potential, thoughts can transform aspirations into tangible realities.

The transformative potential of thoughts manifests in tangible experiences and objects. The conscious direction of thoughts toward our aspirations empowers us to shape the reality we genuinely desire. A lack of awareness in our thought process exposes us to external influences, creating negative thinking patterns that give rise to self-doubt, anxiety, and depression.

A proactive approach involves actively choosing to focus on positive thoughts and affirmations, illuminating a brighter perspective on life and attracting favourable outcomes – **we are designed to be the masters of destiny.** We are the reapers of our harvest! It behoves us to know that circumstances don't mould us, we mould our circumstances, eccentric as it may sound.

Affirmations, positive statements deliberately crafted to influence the subconscious mind, emerge as powerful tools in this cognitive landscape. They aid in reprogramming negative or limiting beliefs and thoughts, replacing them with empowering and constructive ones. Every time I have a negative thought, I knuckle wrap myself and utter 'I delete that thought!' It works exceptionally well for staying on track.

While the plethora of existing literature explores manifestation, creation, and the power of positive thinking on the external world, **the focus on harnessing the vitality of thought for physical health and self-healing remains relatively understated.**

Through introspection and mindful communion with the self, the inherent power of thought can be utilized to promote well-being and embark on a journey of complete self-renewal. Amid external distractions, cultivating awareness and presence in our thoughts entails a profound examination of internal experiences, directing our focus to thoughts and feelings for a deeper connection with ourselves.

Self–reflection and Communion

Descartes coined the philosophical statement "I think, therefore I am." At its core, the statement means the ability to think and reason is proof of our existence. Descartes arrived at this conclusion by radically doubting all of his beliefs and knowledge, including his existence. He realized that even if everything else he believed to be true was false, the fact that he was doubting and thinking was evidence that he existed. Therefore, consciousness and self-awareness are fundamental to our existence as human beings. It also suggests that our thoughts are essential to our identity and that they are what define us as individuals.

"I think, therefore I am" highlights the importance of critical thinking and selfawareness. It reminds us that our thoughts and consciousness are what make us who we are and that we should never take them for granted. If our thoughts are the makers of what we are, then with conscious harnessing and directing, they can lead us to gain mastery over ourselves. Your thoughts shape your character, physical health, behaviour, and ultimately your circumstances. **They act as powerful sculptors and influencers that mould and direct the course of your life.**

Self-reflection is the intimate act of looking inward and examining your thoughts, feelings, and behaviours for a deeper understanding of yourself. It involves examining your beliefs, values, motivations, strengths, and weaknesses with an honest mindset. Through self-reflection, you can identify areas for personal growth, gain clarity on your aspirations and priorities, and improve your overall well-being.

Communion with the self is a sacred process of actively recognising and connecting with your inner being or essence - your silent partner. By tuning in to the inner self, you gain intimacy with your silent chant at a deeper sense of self-awareness. This leads to inner peace, unadulterated silence, and clarity, paving the way for inward coherence when the mind and different parts of the body are in alignment.

The concept of inward coherence has been recognized and emphasized in many ancient spiritual traditions and scriptures, each with its unique practices and approaches towards achieving this state of alignment between the mind and body. This is followed by gently uttered affirmations to the self, focusing attention on a particular state of the self, related to the mind, body, or an external situation. Communion with the self is a powerful tool for personal growth and self-improvement and its efficacy is only known by experiencing.

Self-healing, a significant benefit of the practice of communion with self, emerges from the conviction that thoughts and affirmations can generate vibrations, felt as rivers running in the body, powerful enough to invoke healing. It is rooted in the belief that we can heal ourselves from within. By taking control of our thoughts and learning to harness the power of our minds with equanimity, we can unlock the ability to heal ourselves from physical, emotional, and mental ailments.

Self-healing works by activating the body's natural healing mechanisms. When sick or in pain, our bodies are in a state of imbalance. Self-healing techniques help restore balance by reducing stress, promoting relaxation, and stimulating the immune system. Hand gestures, known as 'mudras' in regular yoga practice, can promote the effectiveness of the immune system. Being free of fear and anxiety creates a positive mindset, enhancing the body's ability to heal itself.

Placing attention on the area of pain or discomfort and simultaneously holding your breath for as long as possible is vital to self-healing. Self-healing during communion with the self involves accessing and acknowledging emotional or physical pain or discomfort and working towards releasing it. Techniques include deep breathing, visualization, and positive affirmations. During meditation or mindfulness, you may focus on a particular area of the body experiencing pain or tension, breathing deeply, and visualizing the area becoming relaxed. Repeating positive affirmations related to healing and well-being enhances overall well-being and works towards healing any emotional or physical pain.

The Potent Swathes of Thought

Thought is accepted as an integral part of the mind in various ancient scriptures and spiritual teachings and traditions.

Buddha said, **"The mind is everything. What you think you become"** Our thoughts bear a creative force that can shape our future, and by changing our thoughts, we can change our reality and become the person we want to be. **Your thoughts are a blueprint of your character.**

The ancient Indian Sage, Vyasaji, known for his spiritual teachings, wrote in Bhagavad Gita, Chapter 6, verse 5, "One must deliver himself with the help of his mind, and not degrade himself. The mind is the friend of the conditioned soul, and his enemy as well" This notion emphasises the importance of self-reliance and self-motivation in mastery over one's destiny rather than dependency on gurus and teachers for validation and guidance.

A verse in the Holy Bible says, **"For as he thinks within himself, so he is"** emphasising the power of thought in shaping our actions and character.

Similarly, many other sacred writings and philosophical traditions place importance on the nature and potency of thought in cultivating a virtuous life.

We are equipped with the ability to generate astounding outcomes by recognising the potency of self-affirming thoughts and suggestions to become makers of ourselves.

The events of our lives are not random, but rather they are influenced by the law of thought vibration. By being mindful of our thoughts and intentionally choosing to focus on positive outcomes, we can shape our reality and create a life that is aligned with our deepest desires and aspirations. We exit the state of reactivity, refusing to assign blame to anyone or any circumstance for our experiences. Our thoughts hold immense power, serving as energetic entities capable of igniting subtle connections and reconciliation with others through simple yet profound phrases such as *"the spirit in me honours the spirit in you,"* silently directed towards individuals during challenging moments. This signifies a profound inner state characterized by heightened vitality and a sense of aliveness, as we immerse ourselves in soothing thoughts.

In the realm of my thoughts, I pulsate with immense vitality. The spirit in me holds a sacred reverence for the spirit within you, and I find myself extending forgiveness to you on instinct, even before any offence transpires. This, to me, is the embodiment of sanctity.

Within the preceding quote is the mental landscape of a profound recognition of the sacredness inherent in every individual - a deep acknowledgement of the spirit residing within oneself and others. It reflects a spiritual reverence for the essence that dwells within each person, setting aside superficial interactions to tap into a deeper understanding of the interconnectedness of all beings. This wisdom empowers us to extend pre-emptive forgiveness, even before any offence occurs, validating the inherent power within us to foster reconciliation and harmony.

Sanctity arises from a deeper connection with one's spirit and a compassionate acknowledgement of the shared spiritual essence in others, giving rise to forgiveness and understanding at a deep level.

As you cultivate inner poise and confidence, your life will transform in extraordinary ways. Your mind not only influences your body but also resonates with other like-minded individuals. By consciously choosing to focus on uplifting thoughts and engaging in self-reflection, meditation, mindfulness, and practising mudras, you can harness the power of your thoughts to promote healing and abundance. The cultivation of a virtuous mindset can bring about profound transformation in your life, enabling you to manifest your dreams and aspirations.

The greatest aspiration for humans, who have remarkably explored space on the one hand and the atom on the other, may now be to embark on an inner journey of self-exploration and emotional regulation. Sadly, we often struggle in this aspect of life, even though we understand that our emotions stem chiefly from our thoughts, beliefs, perceptions, and attitudes.

By exerting control over and directing our thoughts toward regulating our emotions, we can significantly improve our well-being and contribute to the promotion of harmony.

7th Virtue

UNLOCK YOUR POTENTIAL FOR LEADERSHIP

Strive to live a life of
unimpeachable rectitude and integrity.
True joy is not in attaining personal goals but in service for
the greater good of humanity and life on this planet.

Leadership, at its core, is not confined to positions of authority but is a dynamic force that resides within each individual. Let this force help explore the facets of leadership embedded in your character and unlock the latent potential that can propel you to guide and inspire others.

Whether you find yourself in a formal leadership role or aspire to lead from within, this virtue delves into the principles and practices that can elevate your ability to influence, motivate, and create positive change. Prepare to unravel the secrets to becoming a leader who not only excels in external accomplishments but also has a profound impact on the growth and well-being of others.

The potential for wisdom and leadership within every human is boundless, yet often it remains dormant beneath layers of societal conditioning and self-doubt. To unlock this vast potential, you need to boldly delve into the recesses of your mind, and confront fears and any negative preconceptions through uplifting affirmations of self-worthiness. Discovering your true purpose is paramount for a sense of direction aligned with your deepest values and beliefs.

Drawing upon timeless wisdom passed down through the ages, we recognize the interdependencies of all beings and acknowledge our shared responsibility to shape a better world. Only then can we fully harness the power of our potential, leaving an enduring impact on the world and inspiring others to do the same.

It's crucial to remember that our world encompasses not only the physical environment but also more importantly the people we interact with daily, the organizations we belong to, and the legacy we leave behind. It becomes our duty to unlock our potential and contribute to a positive difference in our world, regardless of its scale.

Only those who place the greater good over personal interest can truly lead.

This notion underscores the essence of selfless leadership, where the welfare of the community or nation takes precedence over individual ambitions. Examining this principle through the lens of the current Indian Prime Minister, Narendra Modi, provides an interesting perspective. Modi's leadership style is invariably characterized by a focus on larger societal objectives rather than personal gains. Throughout his tenure, he has spearheaded initiatives aimed at the socio-economic development of India, such as Swachh Bharat Abhiyan (Clean India Mission), Make in India, and Pradhan Mantri Jan Dhan Yojana (financial inclusion program), among others. These initiatives reflect an overarching commitment to the betterment of the nation and the well-being of its citizens. However, opinions on Modi's leadership style may vary, and critics may argue that certain policies or decisions have been politically motivated. Nevertheless, his broader approach suggests an alignment with the principal greater good.

The ability to transcend personal interests and work towards collective welfare is a hallmark of unimpeachable leadership, infused with a sense of trust and unity among the populace. In essence, the evaluation of a leader's commitment to the greater good requires a nuanced understanding of their policies, decisions, and long-term impact on the nation.

Leaders who consistently demonstrate a commitment to the well-being and progress of the people they serve tend to leave a lasting legacy and inspire future generations of leaders to follow a similar path.

Characteristics of an Ideal Leader

To aspire to be a leader of tomorrow, one must embrace the wisdom of George Bernard Shaw and recognize their significant purpose in life as a guiding post for future generations. A genuine leader stands out by serving the greater good of humanity and the planet, understanding that power isn't the goal but inspiring and guiding others toward a better future.

The key qualities of a leader include **integrity, empathy, humility, and a willingness** to learn, being rooted in a clear understanding of their values and purpose. Leadership involves personal growth, grasping human nature, and taking bold action. Not made in a university, true leaders of tomorrow must possess inherent qualities that define great leadership, including **a distinctive and charismatic persona, exceptional intuitive abilities, and a keen sense of foresight.** These qualities are often associated with **sentience**, the ability to experience the world subjectively with **heightened consciousness, selfawareness, and the capacity to feel emotions, thoughts, and sensations.**

Leaders with these qualities are archetypal and understand their surroundings deeply and possess an innate ability to foresee events, making them effective and visionary individuals characterized by remarkable traits, each identified with a specific archetype.

Here are eight of them encapsulated in the acronym SENTIENT:

Sanguine and Spiritual

A sanguine individual is widely recognized for their upbeat positivity, enthusiasm, and sociable nature. Brimming with confidence and vibrant certainty, they fearlessly tackle their endeavours, seeing nothing as too challenging or impossible.

A notable example of a spiritual sanguine is His Holiness the 14th Dalai Lama. He embodies the virtues of optimism, simplicity, humility, kindness, selflessness, and warm-heartedness, serving as a living icon of freedom and non-violence — an epitome of Sanguinity.

In the realm of spirituality, these individuals transcend any negative traits often associated with a sanguine personality, such as deceitfulness and lack of dependability.

Their trustworthiness and sincerity stem from viewing themselves as instruments of an esoteric force, guided by a higher purpose rather than personal gain.

For aspiring leaders, internalizing these qualities and embracing the philosophy of kindness, as exemplified by the Dalai Lama, can be a valuable guide on their leadership journey.

Existing unbounded and unshackled

> **"You were born with potential.**
> **You were born with goodness and trust.**
> **You were born with ideals and dreams.**
> **You were born with greatness.**
> **You were born with wings.**
> **You are not meant for crawling, so don't.**
> **You have wings. Learn to use them and fly." – Rumi**

Existing in an unrestrained and liberated state, these individuals tap into their esoteric power to reason, perceive, and think independently. This quality provides them with a distinct advantage as they cultivate their unique "working creed" - a deeply internalized set of beliefs, principles, and opinions that shape their conduct in life. For instance, they might firmly embrace the notion **"as you think, so shall you be,"** incorporating this belief into their consciousness to steer their thoughts and behaviour. See my 'Working Creed' in the final pages of this book. It took me several months of self-reflection to compile it. It has served me well for the past 25 years.

These individuals do not feel compelled to accept hearsay or blindly adhere to traditions. Instead, they exercise discernment, conducting a thorough analysis, reasoning, and understanding, only embracing ideas that align with their convictions. They possess the ability to distinguish authenticity from falsehood or fiction and remain resilient against external influences. They aspire to transcend the limitations of race, religion, colour, creed, titles, nationality, gender, or any divisive label that tends to perpetuate polarized societies. Emotionally liberated, they are not slavishly attached to any idea or object, yet they maintain a profound sense of interconnectedness with everything.

At peace with themselves, they exude strong self-awareness. As the saying goes, **"Take someone who doesn't keep score, who's not looking to be richer, or afraid of losing, who has not the slightest interest even in his personality, he's free."** They often embody a spirit akin to that of Rumi, the 13th-century Persian poet, Islamic scholar, and Sufi mystic known for his insightful poems expounding themes of love, devotion, and the search for meaning in life. Rumi's influence continues to resonate in contemporary literary and artistic works.

Not One of a Million, but One in a Million

To commence, let me share a quote by George Bernard Shaw that encapsulates his life's purpose: *"This is the true joy in life - being used for a purpose recognized by yourself as a mighty one, being a true force of nature instead of a feverish, selfish little clod of ailments and grievances complaining that the world will not devote itself to making you happy."* Individuals like Shaw, the iconic Irish poet, reformer, and playwright, stand out remarkably. Their lives revolve around selflessness, sacrifice, and the betterment of humanity. They possess a clear purpose in life, guided by their principles and beliefs. Unafraid to tread unconventional paths, they consistently listen to their intuition and remain true to themselves. **"Society does not owe me a living"** serves as their steadfast motto.

Trusting by Nature

Inherently trusting, they firmly believe that trust is the life-sustaining indispensable element; life itself would be unsustainable without it. Upholding the principle of **"trust before being trusted,"** they understand that to earn others' trust, they must consistently demonstrate trustworthiness in every aspect of their conduct and character.

Their natural inclination is to trust others, even if it means risking potential loss by being too trusting too quickly. Prioritizing trust in others, they seek positive and efficient outcomes in their daily interactions. Trust, as the sap of life, forms the foundation they rely on to connect with others, serving as a binding agent for seamless and successful interactions. Proficient in building connections through trust, their trusting nature bears scientifically validated benefits, producing more oxytocin - a hormone for social bonding and trust - in the brain of the trusted person.

Like numerous ancient structures built all around the world, the Brooklyn Bridge in New York City serves as a notable representation of trust. This iconic suspension bridge, spanning the East River to connect Manhattan and Brooklyn, was built in the late 1800s - a colossal engineering project for its time.

Constructing the bridge demanded trust and collaboration among diverse individuals, including the designer, engineers, and construction workers. Successful completion required a foundation of trust, mutual respect, and a shared commitment to the project's success. Today, the Brooklyn Bridge stands as a powerful symbol of trust and connection, underscoring the crucial role bridges play in uniting people and communities. It, like many others in the world, transcends being merely a physical structure; it is a compelling metaphor for the significance of trust in constructing strong and enduring relationships.

In sync with the Authentic Self

Being in sync with the authentic self involves acknowledging that every individual is endowed with a unique inner aspect, often referred to as the silent chant, acting as a connection to the Universe. This authentic self is considered our purest and most untainted part, serving as a guide and conduit for connecting with anyone or anything, anywhere. It provides the resilience to withstand negative external forces and attract positive outcomes. Those who are sentient inherently grasp this power within them and remain aligned with it, setting them apart from those who operate on an ordinary level. This hallmark underscores the significance of embracing and staying connected to one's authentic self to lead a fulfilling and purposeful life.

Renowned American poet and civil rights activist Maya Angelou serves as an exemplary figure in harmony with her authentic self. Throughout her life, Angelou demonstrated an unwavering commitment to speaking her truth and staying true to her values, even in the face of adversity. Her work as a writer and activist was deeply rooted in personal experiences, using her platform to speak out against racism, sexism, and various injustices. Celebrated for the honesty, vulnerability, and authenticity in her poetry and prose, she became a powerful voice for marginalized communities globally. Maya Angelou's legacy continues to inspire people worldwide to live by their authentic selves and to stand up for their beliefs.

Espousing High Mores

To espouse high mores is to embrace and exemplify the unspoken cultural norms of behaviour in various settings, such as home, workplace, and society at large, that stem from shared values.

Individuals who are held in high regard serve as role models of societal expectations and are looked up to as leaders who set a positive example for others to follow. They are the embodiment of acceptable behaviour in all settings, and people often measure themselves against their conduct as a benchmark for their actions.

Throughout his life, Nelson Mandela demonstrated an unwavering commitment to high moral standards and ethical principles. He refused to compromise his values, even in the face of intense pressure and persecution from the apartheid regime. He believed in the power of forgiveness and reconciliation, and he worked tirelessly to promote peace and understanding between different racial and ethnic groups. Mandela's moral leadership and integrity earned him widespread respect and admiration both within South Africa and around the world.

No urge to lead, people just follow them

Possessing the knack for effortless leadership, the leader of tomorrow distinguishes themselves by the absence of a desire to lead driven by personal ambition or competition. Their focus lies in personal growth and promotion of harmonious coexistence with others, endorsing social principles like peaceful coexistence, mutual respect, cooperation, forbearance, and shared responsibility. They prioritize understanding oneself and aligning with societal values for the collective betterment, disavowing the pursuit of personal gain or power. Consequently, they naturally attract followers drawn to their authentic and principled leadership approach.

Mother Teresa exemplified humility and selflessness, leaving an indelible impact through her tireless efforts to provide food, shelter, and medical care to those in need. Despite lacking formal leadership training or personal ambition, she garnered an appeal from people due to her innate compassion and unwavering dedication, inspiring many to emulate her example. Mother Teresa showcased the influential concept of leading through service to others, sparking a global movement of volunteers and organizations dedicated to aiding the less fortunate.

Talented to create by design, not default

Inherently creative and purposeful, the leader of tomorrow disavows the notion of leaving success to chance or circumstance. Instead, they nurture deliberate and purposeful qualities, possessing a clear vision and an unwavering belief in their capacity to drive change. Steering clear of default actions or habits, they approach their endeavours with intention and design. Commencing with a visualization of the desired outcome, they meticulously work towards materializing it, applying their talents to effect positive change in the world.

Understanding their role as instruments of nature, they acknowledge that significant and transformative actions manifest through them. **Steve Jobs** exemplified the talent to create by design, not default. Renowned for his exceptional design sensibility, Jobs had a knack for developing products that were not only technologically innovative but also visually striking and intuitively userfriendly. He staunchly believed in the power of design to enhance people's lives, passionately crafting products that seamlessly merged beauty with functionality. Jobs masterfully cultivated a fiercely loyal customer base devoted to Apple's products and brand.

A visionary leader, he inspired his team to think beyond conventional boundaries and redefine possibilities. Jobs stands as a prime example of an individual who harnessed creativity by design, not default, leveraging his talents to radically transform the world.

The above eight outstandingly striking characteristics are encapsulated in the acronym SENTIENT.

The challenges for tomorrow's leader

The leader of tomorrow must encompass various qualities, serving as a teacher, influencer of consciousness, and reformer of thinking. Their commitment should extend beyond material life and economic advancement, emphasizing the inner essence. As a teacher, the leader should proficiently impart knowledge and skills, offering mentorship and guidance for personal and professional growth. Acting as an influencer of consciousness involves inspiring followers to embrace new perspectives, and shaping the collective mindset for revolutionary change. Similarly, being a reformer of thinking necessitates challenging the status quo, promoting innovative approaches, and fearlessly questioning conventional wisdom. Embracing the inner essence means living with abundant zeal for a vibrant and charismatic life, surpassing any pursuit of material gains.

By doing so, a leader creates a more fulfilling and meaningful environment for their followers. Hence, the leader of tomorrow must embody these qualities - acting as a teacher, influencer of consciousness, and reformer of thinking - while placing the inner essence over materialism and economic advancement.

Chiefly, the challenges lie in emphasising human mental, emotional, and spiritual conditioning over external societal conditions, such as poverty, social deprivation, conflict, disease, and environmental issues, at every level of human endeavour. They must be prepared to contend with discombobulating situations, some examples of which are considered below:

Investing in Future Generation - *"What is your contribution to my future aside from the immense inheritance you have in store for me?"* A grandchild's inquiry about a grandparent's contribution to their future, beyond inheritance, necessitates a thoughtful response that delves into conscience. This conversation can be challenging, requiring a grandparent with a broad perspective and the courage to discuss deep issues. While grandparents naturally aspire to leave a sound legacy for their descendants, tomorrow's leaders must also contemplate their noble contributions to the world or their family's well-being, irrespective of age or circumstances. This can encompass sharing wisdom and life lessons, recounting edifying experiences, or simply promoting the value of love for others. Future leaders should emphasize the importance of creating a more inclusive and compassionate world. To ensure that their grandchildren view it as an inspiring storybook to share and reflect upon, rather than merely accumulating wealth to be wasted or seeking an escape from life's challenges, tomorrow's grandparents should base their lives on this goal.

Reconnecting Today's Youth with Traditional Values - The current generation of youth is growing up in a world that is fast-paced and ever-changing, exposed to an array of technological advancements and luxuries that enhance their lives with ease and convenience. Understandably, this has given rise to a culture of instant gratification and consumerism, where material possessions and shortterm pleasures often take precedence over considering the long-term consequences of their actions. While this lifestyle may hold immediate appeal, it's crucial to recognize its potential to lead to a lack of purpose and direction in life. The traditional values of hard work, perseverance, and discipline that were deeply ingrained in previous generations appear to be fading away. The leader of tomorrow bears a moral responsibility to guide the youth towards these enduring values and wisdom.

Contextualizing the Significance of Personal Contributions - To inspire others and drive meaningful change, the future leader must possess the skill of placing individual efforts into a broader context. This involves grasping the meaning of "the world" concerning any aspirations to make a difference. Without this comprehension, individuals may shy away from ambitious goals that appear overwhelming on a global scale.

The term "the world" should be seen as encompassing those with whom one interacts daily - family, colleagues at work, members of society, and those encountered recreationally – rather than distant nations or societies.

Understanding the context and impact of personal endeavours is paramount for effective leadership. It enables a leader to articulate their vision and mission clearly, ensuring that followers grasp the importance of their roles in achieving collective goals. By emphasizing the interconnectedness of individual efforts, a leader can nurture a sense of community and collegiate existence among their followers.

Moreover, understanding the context and reach of individual missions and aspirations enables a leader to inspire and motivate others to contribute to a shared vision. By underscoring the significance of individual contributions, a leader can spur them to surpass their roles, resulting in heightened innovation, collaboration, and creativity.

Therefore, the leader of tomorrow must possess a comprehensive understanding of the context and impact of individual endeavours, effectively communicating this insight for a sense of collective responsibility and a shared vision.

Shaping a Better World with "Your World" - Forging a potent catalyst for change necessitates coherence that can be harnessed to shape a positive social environment infused with a spirit of cooperation, mutual respect, and peaceful coexistence.

Mahatma Gandhi's quote, "You must be the change you wish

to see in your world." underscores the crucial role of personal responsibility in building a better world.

In the context of influencing "the world" within our daily reach, this quote urges us to initiate positive changes within ourselves and our immediate surroundings. This entails enhancing our behaviour, attitudes, and relationships with those around us, along with participating in community efforts to address issues impacting our daily lives.

By taking these small steps toward positive change, we initiate a ripple effect that can spread a positive influence across the broader world. This is where effective coherence becomes pivotal.

Effective coherence suggests that when people unite towards a common goal, their collective impact surpasses individual efforts. Collaborating with others who share our values and beliefs allows us to magnify our positive influence and bring about more substantial change. For instance, advocating environmental sustainability can commence by reducing our carbon footprint, such as minimizing unnecessary air and sea travel, and encouraging our immediate community to follow suit. By engaging with local environmental groups and initiatives, we can connect with like-minded individuals championing collaborative efforts to effect change on a larger scale. As more people join this movement, our positive influence extends across the wider world, forming a formidable force for change.

"You must be the change you wish to see in your world" stresses the significance of personal responsibility in forging a better world. Through small steps toward positive change in our daily lives and collaborative efforts with others, we set off a ripple effect that propels a positive influence across the broader world.

Instilling Spiritual Consciousness in Future Generations - One of the most profound challenges for the leader of tomorrow is instilling spirituality in the coming generations. Whether in the role of a parent, sibling, mentor, or guru, the leader must serve as a guiding force for the youth of tomorrow, who often grapple with finding purpose and meaning in life.

Spirituality, at its core, involves a greater sense of purpose quelling one's ego and connection with a higher power. It extends beyond individual concerns, embracing the collective and emphasizing the interrelatedness of all beings and the universe.

To nurture spirituality in the youth of tomorrow, the leader must assist them in breaking out of the notion of the 'cocoon of my world' and encourage them to perceive themselves as integral parts of the broader universe with reverence towards it, coaxing them to view it as a living organism deserving of respect and care. Crucially, the leader must instil a sense of greater self-worth and motivate the youth to commune with the universe through stilling themselves and observing silence. By cultivating a deeper connection with the universe, the youth will be better equipped to contend with life's challenges, particularly in the realms of relationships, addictions, and mental health and exemplify the qualities of leaders in making.

Additionally, the leader must educate the youth about their place and significance in the universe, making them aware that their actions carry consequences not only for themselves but for the world around them. With this awareness, they will grow into being impeccably responsible and accountable towards the environment and the community. This personal transformation will enhance their effectiveness and influence in efforts to build a better world. Moreover, by inspiring others to join their cause, they will set in motion a ripple effect that spreads positive influence across the wider world.

The Shape of Tomorrow's Leader

In essence, the leader of tomorrow will not conform to traditional academic models but will instead be largely self-taught, focusing on life's fundamental aspects and virtues. A true leader possesses charisma, intuition, and foresight, traits associated with sentience, allowing for a deep understanding of surroundings and visionary leadership. While formal education is beneficial, the leader of tomorrow will be defined by innate sagacious humane qualities, courage, and equanimity.

They will be infused with compassion and trust, create coherence and naturally draw others to them. Their impact, initially local, will spread through a ripple effect, going across geographic and cultural boundaries. Armed with these superlative qualities, the leader of tomorrow has the potential to ignite the flames of positive change on a global scale and leave behind a lasting legacy for future generations.

8th Virtue

HARNESS THE POWER OF YOUR MINDSET

A Versatile Mindset

The human mind is a remarkable and multifaceted tool powered by immense potential. However, unlocking and harnessing this power is not a simple task; it requires dedication, perseverance, and a deep sense of purpose. To fully tap into this power, it is crucial to cultivate attitudes, beliefs, and values that resonate with your ideals and core principles.

Living out your ideals is a different proposition; it goes beyond mere lip service and involves translating your beliefs into action and consciously incorporating them into your daily life. Being aligned with your cherished principles, you can make significant strides towards actualizing your goals and progressing in critical aspects of your life, such as finding purpose and meaning.

Building a rock-solid mindset is an ongoing process that requires continuous effort and self-reflection. It entails regularly evaluating and reinforcing the right attitudes and beliefs that shape your perspective. By conscious perseverance in this endeavour, you empower yourself to overcome obstacles and seize opportunities that come your way.

Actively applying the principles ingrained in your working creed is essential for continued personal growth and self-actualization. It means integrating your beliefs into your behaviour, decisions, and interactions with others to enhance your well-being and also inspire and positively influence those around you.

Furthermore, cultivating a purpose-driven mindset allows you to find deeper meaning in life. When you live aligned with your core values, you experience a sense of fulfilment and satisfaction that comes from pursuing what truly matters to you. This sense of purpose acts as a guiding light, directing your actions and choices towards attaining more worthy goals.

A versatile mindset has to be open, creative, and willing to try new approaches to solve problems and seize opportunities. It means adjusting your thinking and behaviour to fit different contexts and being comfortable with life's ambiguities and uncertainties. Ultimately, a versatile mindset enables you to approach situations with flexibility and adaptability, leading to more effective solutions and personal growth.

The legendary Leonardo da Vinci is a fine example of a person with a versatile mind. He was not only a painter but also a scientist, inventor, architect, musician, writer, and engineer. He had a curious mind, always eager to learn and explore new things. His knack for thinking creatively and outside the box helped him come up with innovative ideas and solutions. His versatile mindset allowed him to make significant contributions to art, science, and technology.

"Learning never exhausts the mind." - *Leonardo Da Vinci*

Individuals with a versatile mindset have a clear sense of rectitude and don't let any moral code or emotional blackmail hinder them from doing what they believe is right. They can differentiate between matters of the heart and what is appropriate in a given situation. They are not blindly conforming to societal norms but have the gumption to make their own choices.

"Never let your sense of morals get in the way
of doing what's right." - Isaac Asimov

A virtuous mindset empowers individuals to tap into their inner resources and adapt to changing circumstances. In the face of setbacks or challenges, a person with a virtuous mindset remains resilient. Instead of succumbing to discouragement or defeat, they maintain composure, staying calm, focused, and optimistic. Drawing from their knowledge, skills, and values, they navigate obstacles and uncover innovative solutions.

Their philosophical outlook serves as a wellspring of wisdom and equanimity in various challenging life situations. For example, when confronted with a significant setback, such as financial loss in a new business deal, a person with a virtuous mindset doesn't allow despair or frustration to overwhelm them. Reflective and optimistic, they step back, assess the situation, and extract valuable lessons from the experience.

They leverage their inner resources to stay composed and focused, using their knowledge and wisdom to reframe the situation positively. This may involve identifying new opportunities, devising strategies to recoup losses, or exploring alternative paths aligned with their life's ambitions.

In addition to adapting to changing circumstances, **a virtuous mindset empowers individuals to tap into their subconscious, accessing an inner wellspring of wisdom.** This enables them to draw upon intuition and past experiences, guiding their decisions and actions toward choices that support personal growth and development.

A distinctive strength of those with a virtuous mindset lies in their profound self-awareness and commitment to introspection. Continuously examining their thoughts, intentions, and emotions ensures alignment with their values and principles. This ongoing self-reflection deepens their understanding of personal strengths and weaknesses, enabling them to take appropriate actions in various situations. Habitual introspection and self-reflection serve as manifestations of a perpetual commitment to self-improvement.

Additionally, the awareness of their thoughts and emotions helps such a person to **remain centred and grounded in difficult situations.** They can stay calm and rational, even when faced with adversity or challenges. This is because they have developed a deep understanding of their emotional responses, and have learned to regulate their emotions healthily.

Their self-awareness naturally extends to an awareness of their outer environment and the people around them. By putting themselves in other people's shoes and understanding their perspectives, they become more compassionate and understanding. This empathetic ability helps build strong relationships based on trust and mutual respect.

Maintaining a mindset focused on noble virtues equips individuals to overpower life's challenges with grace, resilience, and creativity. Actively seeking opportunities to help others and make a positive impact in the community allows individuals to harness the power of these virtues, achieving personal fulfilment and contributing to the greater good. Applying these virtues in relationships cultivates empathy and understanding for deeper and more meaningful connections. Ultimately, leveraging the power of a virtuous mindset involves using the ingrained qualities to impact the world around you.

Integrating the Virtuous Mindset in Daily Life

Incorporating a virtuous mindset into our daily lives requires **intention and effort**. It is not enough to simply understand the principles and concepts of virtuous living; we must actively strive to thread them into our thoughts, actions, and habits. **We must become them**.

To begin with, we must identify the areas of our lives where we can apply virtuous values. This could include our relationships with others, our work, our leisure time, and even our internal dialogue. Once we have identified these areas, we instinctively begin to be subsumed in the practice of **kindness, honesty, gratitude, and self-discipline**.

One key aspect of integrating a virtuous mindset into our daily lives is consistency. We must make a conscious effort to honestly apply virtuous values and behaviours, even in situations that are challenging or uncomfortable. Over time, these behaviours will become ingrained in our habits and will come more naturally to us. **We must become them.**

Another important aspect of integrating a virtuous mindset is accountability. We must hold ourselves **accountable for our thoughts and actions**, and be willing to take responsibility when we fall short of our ideals. It is also important to surround ourselves with others who share our commitment to virtuous living, as they can provide support and encouragement on our journey.

Ultimately, integrating a virtuous mindset into our daily lives requires **a commitment to ongoing growth and development.** We must remain open to learning, willing to make mistakes and learn from them, and willing to continually refine and improve our behaviours. Through this ongoing process of growth and development, we maintain a sharpened sense to constructively impact every aspect of our lives.

Here are some rules to personalize and live by:

Honour yourself

Above all **accept yourself for what you are**. Throw your light on the world around you. Know within yourself that you are a gift of nature created for a unique purpose. Trust yourself, believe in yourself, and always act with honour to deliver your purpose. In all circumstances be true to who you are and what you value. Others will respect you and not define you or take away your dignity.

As Robin Sharma said, "Without integrity and honour, having everything means nothing." Honour yourself by respecting your needs, your boundaries, and your dreams. Honour yourself by living with courage, compassion, and authenticity. By honouring yourself, you can increase your self-esteem and poise. Your honour for yourself is your real wealth for it makes you stand tall.

Practise forgiveness

Forgiving is not a sign of meekness or weakness. Forgive both others and yourself for whatever has occurred. Bring to an end the tenancy in your heart of anger, hatred, vengeance, shame and guilt which only weigh upon your spirit. Only complete forgiveness can set you free from the stranglehold of resentment and bitterness and pave the way for "inner unshacklement" for psychological, emotional and spiritual relief. You see, **FORGIVE** is an apt acronym for **"Freeing Ourselves, Releasing Grudges, and Invoking Vibrant Energy."** Inner unshacklement is liberation or freedom from internal constraints, limitations, or burdens that hold a person back. It paves the way for bliss to begin flourishing. As Martin Luther King Jr. eloquently stated, *"Darkness cannot drive out darkness; only light can do that. Hate cannot drive out hate; only love can do that."* Forgiveness, therefore, is not an act of forgetting or condoning wrongdoing; rather, it is a conscious choice to release oneself from the burden of pain and embrace peace. It is an attribute of the big-hearted, signifying the ability to extinguish the flames of bitterness within. Forgiveness is a powerful tool for self-healing, requiring immense emotional stamina and endurance. It goes beyond mere words; it is a profound process of inner cleansing.

However, forgiveness can be challenging, especially in the face of past atrocities committed by authoritarian regimes against certain races, nationalities, or tribes.

The wounds inflicted by such injustices can run deep, making it difficult to forget or forgive. Yet, harbouring resentment only perpetuates fragmentation within communities, hindering efforts to foster harmony and unity.

Moreover, holding onto grudges against long-departed perpetrators of heinous crimes ultimately disconnects individuals from their spiritual essence. It undermines faith in the belief that justice will prevail for all who have suffered. Therefore, true liberation from resentment requires introspection and a willingness to let go of clinging to past grievances. Until then resentment acts as a heavy burden, weighing down upon one's shoulders like an oppressive yoke, impeding their freedom and hindering their ability to move forward with ease and lightness. Only after exterminating resentment can individuals truly embrace the transformative power of forgiveness and pave the way for healing and reconciliation.

To quash any sense of suffering and regain their spiritual essence, individuals have to embrace the ancient spiritual law – **The fault is of the sufferer.** At first glance, this rather oxymoronic-sounding statement does not sink in the mind. But if you accept that **we are as we think** and are, therefore, directly and indirectly, responsible for creating our reality, then it becomes difficult to argue against this wisdom. **The way you think and respond to life can or cannot prevent you from coming out of the mire of suffering. You're the boss!**

A side note: Once during a coffee break at a conference, I happened to be having a sociable chat with a very lady who, out of curiosity, asked me about the secret to my youthful appearance. I responded by explaining that I practise habits such as mindfulness, meditation, and forgiveness, which involves silently forgiving even those, such as Hitler, who have committed heinous crimes. She reacted with disbelief and exclaimed, "Hitler? Never!" before walking away annoyed, and I stood there wondering how deeply resentful she was about a past event. True forgiveness requires a big heart and the willingness to let go of immobilizing anger and resentment. It is a challenging process, but it allows us to move forward and live a more fulfilling life. I sincerely hope that lady has since reflected on forgiving.

Be perpetually grateful.

Gratitude is the treasure you can create perpetually from within and spend freely without fear of bankrupting yourself of it. Without a sense of gratitude, you are incomplete, but with it, you are armed with all you need to nurture your spirit. Be eternally grateful for everything. Explore, experience, accept, affirm and exude life with gratitude; it nourishes your heart and resides in you as an antidote to any agonizing anxiety and worry. Sown within gratitude is the magnetism to attract blessings – **the source of joy and the end of struggle.** When expressing gratitude for the little you have, you find you have more than enough. Somehow gratitude attracts more of everything that you are grateful for, or it just does not exhaust itself. It is a trigger to create optimism and improved self-worth. It can increase feelings of happiness, contentment, and well-being. By focusing on what you have rather than what you lack, you can shift your perspective and find joy in the present moment. Be thankful you were born. Be thankful for every moment, for every bite of food, for each small joy. **You were owed none of this. Everything is a gift.** Expressing gratitude through the grace before a meal transcends a mere perfunctory 'thank you';

it becomes a powerful act that ensures the next meal will be placed on the table.

Choose with an open mind and open heart

Have a mind that is open to everything and beholden to nothing. Let each choice be your own, stand by it, and embrace it with a mindset of curiosity and a thirst for unravelling the unknown. Be receptive to new ideas and perspectives; set aside preconceived notions and consider different viewpoints before making a decision. By approaching choices with an open mind, you can make intentional decisions that align with your life's purpose. Individuals accustomed to living by this ideal tend to be fearless in causing controversy. They remain unruffled and tend not to be discombobulated by most outcomes.

Let your vision guide your actions

When letting your vision guide your actions, your intentions and aspirations are crucial, but they remain meaningless unless you act upon them. Every day, take concrete steps towards realizing your life's purpose. Keep your purpose at the forefront of your mind, and let it shape your decisions and actions. Ensure that your actions align with your values, beliefs, and principles. Let your creed mirror your vision and mission in life, using it as a guide to propel you closer to your goals. Remember that your life's purpose is not a one-time achievement; it's an ongoing journey that demands commitment, dedication, and perseverance.

Suppose you've been struggling with a gambling addiction for several years, knowing that this addiction is causing you financial losses and harming your relationships. Applying personal creed take time to reflect on what you truly value, such as self-esteem, financial stability, healthy relationships, and personal growth. With these values in mind, create an affirmative statement like: *"I am committed to living a life of financial stability, healthy relationships, and personal growth. I am in control of my actions and choices, and I will not let my addiction control me. I choose to prioritize my values over my impulses, taking consistent action towards my goals."* Use this as a guide for your actions, setting specific goals like attending support groups and therapy sessions while avoiding situations triggering your gambling urges. Reach out to loved ones for support and accountability. Over time, your commitment to your creed will help you break free from your addiction and live with high self-esteem.

Revel in your life

Face everything in life with a smile. It means to let your life itself be a source of joy and a song of celebration. Nothing is bigger than to be your light and celebrate your life with all its vicissitudes. Only see nature's splendour wherever you cast your gaze. Don't wait for some special day to celebrate the gift of living, but make each new day a celebration of life. You are breathing and you are alive and you have consciousness, celebrate it with gusto! Know that the force is with you and you are always blessed.

Know unity with Spirit and with all of creation

Understanding and embracing unity with Spirit and all of creation is the first step towards self-realization and the end of struggle. It is a profound recognition that everything in the universe is interconnected and part of the same magnificence. This unity extends beyond ourselves and encompasses the entirety of existence. When we fully grasp this truth, we transcend our limited perspective and perceive the inherent beauty and oneness of all things. From the tiniest atom to the vast expanse of the cosmos, every element of creation is intricately linked. This realization evokes a sense of wonder and reverence and in some way is related, thus rousing us to treat all beings with compassion and kindness.

Recognizing our unity with Spirit and the entirety of creation not only allows us to embrace the graceful choreography of life but also to comprehend our role within it. It is a unifying character trait marked by perpetual serenity, selfdiscovery, and enlightenment.

This journey of harnessing the power of our mindset is an ongoing endeavour that will serve as our guiding companion in every aspect of daily life.

9th Virtue

TAKE STOCK OF YOUR MINDSET

As you progress through 'Being' and 'Doing' to 'Becoming', your journey through life gathers momentum. Your mindset becomes attuned to shaping how you perceive life, face challenges, and pursue goals. Embracing growth in unfoldment, you perceive challenges as gateways to opportunity, effort as the path to mastery, and setbacks as invaluable lessons in the journey of selfrealization. You become resilient, motivated, and open to continuous learning. You take to heart the evolving nature of your attributes, staying mindful of your capacities. Through continuous improvement, your values and inner purity remain steadfast.

Let it be etched within you:
a mind forged in enduring values and inner purity, and
guided by universal principles and courage, is truly virtuous.
Your mind is your Sanctum - your sacred space.

In your cherished Sanctum, reside enduring values - honesty, integrity, compassion, justice, and respect for others. Your deportment reflects sincerity, authenticity, and a genuine desire to do what's right. Preserving inner purity requires self-reflection, self-discipline, and dogged pursuit of new insights.

Upright thinking becomes your toolbox, weaving honesty, fairness, and moral rectitude into every action. Critical analysis, empathy, and ethical decisions are its essence free of deceit or manipulation where only integrity and truthfulness thrive.

You champion universal principles, transcending differences, and sculpting ethical behaviours and moral judgments. With courage and fortitude, you face challenges, acting with conviction even amidst adversity. Upholding these virtues demands commitment, even against the prevailing tide. You exercise selfgovernance, inspiring others with your originality, and contributing to a better world.

> **"How far that little candle throws his beams!**
> **So shines a good deed in a weary world"**
> William Shakespeare - The Merchant of Venice

Innate goodness has to prevail; even a small act of kindness can have a powerful impact on the world, just as a small candle can illuminate a dark room.

You should not underestimate the power of your actions, no matter how small they may seem, as they have the potential to shine a light in the darkness and make a perceptible difference in the world. The world can often seem weary and dark, full of problems and struggles that can leave many overwhelmed and helpless. But even during such difficulties, a simple act of kindness or goodness can have a transformative effect. It inspires hope, brings joy, and offers comfort to those in need.

You radiate by consciously rejecting the societal norms

polluted by what is commonly known as the 'Deadly Sins', the root cause of all human failings, which have emerged from the primal passions viz: **lust, anger, greed, attachment, and vanity**, the Big-5. To augment your spiritual evolution, you remain conscious of these in all your thoughts, words and actions.

The Big 5

These perversions represent distorted thinking that can lead to negative behaviours, detrimental consequences, and a decline in one's well-being. They manifest in various forms and affect different aspects of life. These deadly perversions of the mind are not dormant; they are akin to free radicals in the human body, posing a nuisance and retarding our spiritual growth. They continue to cast shadows upon our lives, hindering our pursuit of eternal bliss.

However, the obstacles we face are not external but located within ourselves. They are the outcomes of our warped thinking and false interpretations of events. Our reactions to them shape our destinies. To combat this internal struggle, we must confront these depravities that have plagued humans and led to morally reprehensible, deviant, and harmful behaviours that obstruct our journey toward inner transformation and moral purity.

Depravity manifests in various forms, including violence, cruelty, dishonesty, avarice, exploitation, and sexual misconduct. Such actions represent a significant departure from the standards of decency and moral righteousness that should guide our lives.

Let us not underestimate the profound impact of these insidious passions. Their pervasive influence has created a global cesspit of mistrust, leading to burdensome processes and procedures that hinder the lives of innocent individuals across all walks of life.

Lust, often misconstrued as a mere desire for sexual gratification, holds deeper spiritual implications. In its true essence, lust manifests when one seeks selfserving fulfilment at the expense of another or to the detriment of others. Acts such as sexual molestation and perverse behaviours certainly embody lust, as they violate the boundaries of consent and inflict undeserved harm upon others.

However, it is crucial to recognize that sexuality, when expressed within the bounds of love and respect, becomes a powerful expression of intimacy. Beyond sexual acts, lust extends to various forms of excessive and obsessive indulgence. The insatiable pursuit of wealth accumulation, the abuse of substances like drugs and alcohol, the compulsive consumption of exotic foods against health advice, the indulgence in explicit literature, and engaging in addictive entertainment such as gambling all fall under the domain of lust.

This kind of spiritless behaviour reflects a regression of the mind's normal functioning into abnormality. In this state, individuals neglect common decency, disregard the well-being and safety of others, and ignore the consequences of their actions.

In the realm of business, extreme lust for profit can drive individuals to callously dismiss employees without compassion or consideration for their livelihoods. Similarly, leaders who misuse their power to eliminate opposition and retain political office demonstrate a form of lust. The ruthless and frenzied slaughter of individuals based on their ethnic differences represents the most abhorrent manifestation of lust. Such extreme forms of lust degrade individuals to the lowest rung of the ladder among all living creatures.

Identifying and recognising the destructive nature of lust is essential for personal growth and the cultivation of virtuous qualities. By overcoming the grip of lust, individuals can redirect their energies towards acts of humanity. It requires a conscious effort to align actions with moral principles and to prioritize the wellbeing and dignity of oneself and others. Only by destroying lust can individuals elevate themselves to a higher plane of existence.

Anger, the destructive force of uncontrolled rage is a passionate force that possesses the capacity to wreak havoc. It manifests itself in various subtle ways, extending beyond mere annoyance or hostility. Frustration, impatience, indifference, and intolerance signify this potent emotion. Moreover, anger manifests as jealousy, envy, gossip, nagging, excessive criticism, and other forms of derogatory remarks aimed at others or oneself. It dwells within each of us, assuming different disguises. The destructive power of anger reveals itself in numerous actions and behaviours. Nagging a spouse or engaging in comparisons to make them feel inadequate, expressing dissatisfaction or frustration through constant fault-finding or attempting to change someone's fundamental nature, displaying callous disregard or indifference towards others, using derogatory language, maliciously damaging property, and even resorting to blatant lies - all these are indicators of anger which also extend in the present time to online harassment and cyberbullying, and aggressive driving and physical altercations on the road.

Anger is a pervasive affliction that defies even the most skilled healers and serves as the root cause of many failures and a great deal of unhappiness in societies. The intricate complexities of anger, with all its negative distortions, cannot be healed through conventional medical means. Instead, the remedy lies in bringing a personal meaning to life by engaging in self-reflection.

This journey of self-discovery and self-regulation holds the key to taming the unruly nature of anger and finding inner peace.

Greed, known as avarice or covetousness, is undeniably a destructive passion with far-reaching consequences. It is characterized by an intense and selfish desire for excessive wealth, power, food, fame, or recognition, often at the expense of spiritual values. A greedy individual becomes consumed by materialistic ambitions, disregarding the importance of a compassionate and humane society.

Operating under a constant scarcity mentality, the greedy place personal gain above all else, even at the cost of harming others. The insidious nature of greed drives individuals to extreme lengths in their pursuit of incessant 'adding more'. They may place their self-interest, wealth, and belongings over the well-being of family and friends, resorting to breaking relationships and lies to protect their interests.

This passion transcends socioeconomic boundaries. It permeates all aspects of society, corrupting individuals of all ages and walks of life. While the wealthy may seek public recognition for their substantial donations, those with limited means may also seek acknowledgement for their philanthropic acts, both driven by the expectation of personal returns.

It rears its ugly head in various forms, such as a person making a significant financial contribution to a political party in exchange for favours, a pharmaceutical company paying a research analyst an exorbitant sum to write an embellished report on a new drug for promotional purposes, a retail shop owner dishonestly manipulating cash registers and underreporting earnings to evade taxes, or a customs official accepting bribes to allow the entry of prohibited narcotics into a country.

These acts of greed erode all foundations of trust and integrity. Moreover, greed lies at the heart of bribery and corruption, infiltrating cultures and institutions. When the desire to accumulate wealth and gain a reputation from positions of privilege and trust takes hold, individuals may compromise accepted standards of ethical behaviour, jeopardizing entire industries and economic systems.

The consequences of greed extend beyond personal gain and can have devastating effects on nations as a whole. For instance, consider a politician who promises to reduce taxes to gain political power. Once elected, they follow through on their promise, but to balance the budget, crucial government expenditures in areas such as healthcare, prisons, and education are cut.

As a result, hospitals struggle to provide adequate care, and individuals with serious mental disorders are left untreated and roaming the streets. Any compromised prison security leads to drug infiltration and escapes, and underfunded schools suffer from a lack of resources and qualified teachers. The long-term impact of compromised healthcare, security, and education corrodes an entire nation's well-being and prospects.

Quite obviously, greed significantly threatens societal harmony, ethical standards, and collective progress. This passion thwarts the cultivation of a virtuous mindset and can infiltrate the human psyche eroding moral principles. It thrives in the dark recesses of selfish desires and insatiable ambitions. Unlike a physical ailment with a medical remedy, greed cannot be cured through conventional means. It is a pervasive characteristic that feeds the metaphorical cockroaches within us. It creeps into the very DNA of life, spreading its destructive influence and driving individuals to amass wealth at any cost. It is the worst form of ingratitude for the Maker giving sway to widespread apathy, indifference and disaffectedness amongst innocent masses.

To combat greed, one must embrace an altruistic mentality characterised by selfreform, introspection, and a quest for meaning and purpose. It requires a shift in perspective, a conscious effort to detach from the allure of material possessions and societal validation.

Only by recognizing the true value of integrity, generosity, and the interconnectedness of all beings can we break free from the grips of greed. Let us remember that greed, much like the persistence of cockroaches, can only be conquered through a collective effort of self-examination, personal growth, and a commitment to building a world where the light of compassion, fairness, and shared prosperity outshines the darkness of insatiable desires that are causing the ever-widening rift between the rich and poor in the world.

Attachment, a pervasive passion that silently takes hold of our hearts and minds, has the power to bind us in invisible chains. It manifests in various forms, from our attachment to material possessions and identities to our attachment to relationships, work, and even ideologies. Unbeknownst to us, it shackles our souls, hindering our spiritual growth and preventing us from reaching our full potential.

The grip of attachment is often masked as a sense of security, but in reality, it engenders fear - fear of losing what we hold dear, fear of change, and fear of the unknown. This fear-driven attachment stifles our natural talents and stifles the free flow of energy and creativity within us. We become preoccupied with protecting and preserving what we have, sacrificing the freedom to explore and embrace new possibilities. Our attachment extends its reach into every aspect of our lives.

Our homes once meant to be sanctuaries, become fortresses as we meticulously safeguard our possessions, installing elaborate security systems and purchasing insurance.

Our attachment to material belongings robs us of the joy of simplicity and leaves us burdened by the weight of excessive accumulation.

Similarly, our attachment to status and reputation at work breeds a constant fear of failure and the need to guard our position at all costs. We hold tightly to our knowledge and methods, fearing that sharing them would render us replaceable. This mentality hampers collaboration, growth, and the exchange of ideas that can propel us forward collectively.

Even in matters of faith and belief, attachment can distort our understanding and lead to rigid dogmas and divisions. We cling to our religious or ideological identities, branding them as

119

ours and feeling compelled to defend them, even at the expense of compassion, understanding, and harmony.

The consequences of attachment are far-reaching, filling our lives with clutter, both physical and mental. The accumulation of possessions and the obsession with reputation and status create barriers that confine and restrict us. We become trapped within the confines of our attachments, unable to experience the liberation that comes from letting go.

To break free from the chains of attachment, we must cultivate a mindset of total abandon understanding that true freedom lies not in possessing everything but in possessing nothing - not even ourselves. It is about cultivating the mind to see yourself as a stakeholder in the Universe and thus seeing the futility of claiming ownership of or possessing anything.

It is through the practice of letting go, embracing impermanence, and finding contentment within, that we can liberate ourselves from the burdens of attachment and open ourselves to a more expansive and fulfilling existence. Embarking on the journey of releasing our attachments, simplifying our lives, and creating space for growth, love, and genuine connections dismantle the prison walls of possessiveness, thus creating a sense of inner freedom and living with open hearts, minds, and spirits.

Vanity, the fifth and most perilous of the passions, ensnares us in a web of selfdeception and illusion on the journey of worldly education and personal growth.

It begins to take shape when we start perceiving ourselves as separate and superior beings, measuring our worth against the appearances, possessions, and achievements of others. In our quest for distinction, we may seek cultural superiority, lay claim to prestigious ancestral backgrounds, or seek fleeting connections with renowned individuals to elevate our status. We become consumed by the desire to project an image of wealth, superiority, or accomplishment, using it as the sole means to validate our self-worth.

Beneath this façade lie layers of fear, insecurity, and a deep sense of inadequacy. These individuals lack a profound understanding of life's deeper essence, rendering their thoughts shallow and devoid of genuine energy. They reside in a shallow world of make-believe, where what is visible holds more significance than what is invisible. The external appearance takes precedence over character and values, and the pursuit of youthfulness through artificial means outweighs the importance of holistic well-being. Living in perpetual pretence, they surrender their true selves and exist on borrowed identities. Their lives become a performance, a constant need to uphold a defensive front. Their very existence depends on the validation and favourable opinions expressed by others, feeding their souls with fleeting nourishment.

Like a river swollen with monsoon rains, marvelling at its grandeur, vanity engulfs individuals in a false sense of their significance. They bask in the illusion of invincibility, believing they can overcome any obstacle. However, just as the river humbly merges into the vastness of the sea without a whimper, vanity too meets the ultimate reality. Imagine a river perceiving its expansive breadth, flowing forcefully, with the power to bring down bridges and carry mighty ships. It revels in its majesty, unaware of its transience. Yet, when it meets the boundless sea, it is humbled and dissolved without a trace.

Similarly, vanity blinds us to the profound and eternal forces of nature that remind us of our fleeting existence. In the grand matrix of life, individuals come and go like particles of dust in a sunbeam passing through a tiny air vent. Vanity masks the truth, obscuring our connection to the greater whole.

To dismantle the mask of vanity, we must embark on a journey of self-discovery and embrace the dynamic nature of our existence. We must recognize the transitory nature of appearances and achievements and turn inward to cultivate a genuine sense of self-worth rooted in character, integrity, and the realization of our interconnectedness with all life. By relinquishing the illusory self and embracing the divinity of authenticity, we can unveil the mask and rediscover our true essence in harmony with the vastness of existence.

These inescapable base tendencies have evolved and intertwined with the complexities of our modern world. With each passing era, new manifestations of these primal passions, the Deadly Sins, have emerged encompassing technology, social interactions, and cultural shifts.

Recognizing and addressing these demons within is integral to cultivating a virtuous mindset.

Emerged from the over-arching Big-5, here are a few key Deadly Sins characterized by behaviours and tendencies of corporations, businesses and individuals:

Unbridled and insatiable pursuit of wealth accumulation without commensurate effort or creating value, resorting to fraudulent schemes, price gouging, creating and concealing fortuitous windfall gains, evading taxes, or engaging in deceptive methods to exploit and gain from public programs, all encompassed by greed and lust.

Misapplication of intellect and knowledge where alignment with universally accepted tenets is lacking, misuse of knowledge and training to perpetrate cybercrime, financial crime against the public, and such misdeeds disregarding any thoughts of fairness, compassion, loyalty, kindness, and dignity, all seen as unadulterated greed.

Harbouring hatred on racial, ethnic, tribal or any such grounds, which is all a manifestation of prejudice and discrimination stemming from ignorance, fear, and a distorted sense of superiority or entitlement. It nurtures and perpetuates negative attitudes, biases, and animosity towards individuals or groups based on their racial, ethnic, or tribal identity. This base practice is not born out of an inherent trait but a learned behaviour. It leads to the marginalisation, dehumanisation, and mistreatment of individuals and communities perpetuating cycles of violence, conflict, and injustice. This depravity breeds division, prejudice, and societal unrest, hindering the progress and harmony of diverse societies.

Nurturing such hatred not only inflicts wounds on its targets but also corrodes the souls of its bearers. It blinds them to the intrinsic value and common humanity of every individual, robbing them of the chance to celebrate the vibrant tapestry of diversity. This toxic sentiment erects barriers to genuine connections, isolates individuals, and undermines the very fabric of social coherence.

Overcoming this deadly sin requires conscious introspection to challenge and unlearn deeply ingrained biases and prejudices.

Unrestrained advancement and application of science that is leading to replacing human effort with machines and man-made intelligence, disregarding the potential enslavement of humanity to technology and the harmful effects of a spiritless, materialistic society where deeper thought to enlarge the mind and consciousness are relegated to irrelevance.

This unbridled advancement of science is a step toward consigning to the waste bin the notion that 'there is no power greater than the Intelligence of Nature, the source of our existence'.

Unconscionable indulgence in excessive pleasure that is tantamount to the waste of a society's resources. It is typified by behaviours such as flaunting personal wealth and engaging in excessive, crass or extreme activities solely for the pursuit of pleasure or fame without regard for moral principles, moderation, or the well-being of oneself or others. Such individuals place immediate gratification and personal enjoyment above all else. Abuse of harmful or injurious substances, hazardous activities, compulsive gambling or pursuits that go beyond what is considered reasonable or socially acceptable are the key characteristic traits of these insatiable acts that see no ethical or moral boundaries. Of particular note is an addiction to pornography and sexual content, accessed readily on the internet, which leads to unbridled consumption of explicit material that has permeated not only personal lives but also workplaces, giving rise to a widespread objectification of individuals and unhealthy sexual behaviours.

> **Most of the luxuries, and many of the**
> **so-called comforts of life**
> **are not only dispensable,**
> **but positive hindrances to the elevation of mankind.**
> *- Henry David Thoreau*

Your mind on the virtuous path discerns and distances itself from much of the reprehensible behaviour witnessed in modern times imputed to one or more of these deadly sins.

Actions, where goodness and compassion prevail, will pave the way for embarking on the ultimate phase: '**The Powerhouse of Becoming**'

THE BECOMING PHASE

*In the crucible of transformation,
we forge the steel of our spirit and
sculpt the masterpiece of our destiny.*

10th Virtue

YOUR MINDSET – THE POWERHOUSE OF BECOMING

Taking to heart the certainty of dying makes living
a noble cause worth dying for with dignity.

You are now embarking on the culminating phase of this evolutionary journey – 'The Powerhouse of Becoming.' As you step into these final chapters, a deep realization dawns from the introspective voyage through **Being** and **Doing** that brokenness and fragmentation - a state of 'dis-memberment' – is the underlying source of all disaffection, estrangement, and suffering. However, in the vibrancy of **Becoming**, the process of 're-memberment' will unfold to guide you back to the awareness of your origin as a **spirit being**. Here, amid the unfolding chapters, you'll unveil the dormant facets of your potential, each revelation akin to a dormant powerhouse waiting to be activated within you. Fragmentation will give way to wholeness as you emerge as a re-membered holistic being.

"The gift of mental power comes from God, a divine
being, and if we concentrate our minds on that
truth, we become in tune with this great power"
-Nikola Tesla

Nikola Tesla suggests that mental power is a divine gift
bestowed upon us by a higher source, often referred to as God
or a divine being. This gift of mental power is a profound
aspect of our being, enabling us to explore the depths of our
consciousness and realise our limitless potential.

To fully harness this gift, it is important to embrace the
truth that **our mental power comes from a higher source,** and
we need to attune ourselves to this great power. Our mindset is
the conduit connecting us to the vast reservoir of mental energy
within and around us.

Now, the notion 'Your Mindset - The Powerhouse of
Becoming,' takes on a new dimension. It becomes the key to
unlocking our true potential and embarking on a journey of
self-realization and unfoldment.

By adopting a growth-oriented mindset and trusting the
process of becoming, we can tap into the divine gift of mental
powers within us. We become more attuned to the divine
essence within us and gain a deeper understanding of our true
selves. This mindset allows us to overcome limiting beliefs, fears,
and self-doubt, thus empowering us to explore new possibilities
and reach the heights we once thought unattainable. Initially,
embarking on this journey may seem daunting, challenging
our trust in its potential. Yet, as we embrace it wholeheartedly,
we will make it our own, nurturing the growth of trust within
ourselves.

Our mindset can also be a gateway to a higher state of consciousness, enabling us to access a wellspring of creativity, wisdom, and inspiration. It is through this powerful mindset that we can manifest our dreams, connect with our purpose, and design a life of our choice.

Let Tesla's message about the gift of mental power and its divine origins resonate deeply with the central theme of 'Your Mindset - The Powerhouse of Becoming.'

Now it is the beginning of your extraordinary spiritual quest – embark on a journey of self-realization that delves into the depths of existence, uncovering hidden truths, spiritual concepts, mystical experiences, and metaphysical wonders. Your Mindset sets ablaze this evolutionary odyssey propelling you towards self-mastery.

You already know through the 'Being' and 'Doing' phases that within you lies the incredible power to transcend mere beliefs and venture into a realm of elevated possibilities. You will hone your possessed potential to unlock the gateway to a higher level of existence that will ignite the fires of personal evolution. Your mindset will lead you to discover your unique self and you will become the very best version of yourself - **a highly evolved being** - that thrives on the understanding that you are a microcosm of the universe and so, the universe is in you as well as you are in the universe. This knowing of connectedness is the fuel that propels your unfoldment exponentially. Your mindset will wield the power to mould your perceptions of the world, exert influence over how you confront challenges, seize opportunities, and traverse life's intricate pathways with a sense of calm nonchalance. Gradually your thoughts, attitudes and actions will reflect the aura of one who has attained self-mastery.

Self-mastery is the art of gaining control over every facet of oneself. It calls for heightened self-awareness, unwavering discipline, and a deep comprehension of one's inner mechanisms and recurrent patterns. This expedition requires an unwavering dedication to a life marked by personal evolution and characterised by equanimity, emotional acumen, and a laser-sharp sense of purpose.

At its core, self-mastery empowers you to make conscious choices. You will instinctively begin to de-clutter your mind as you begin to live mindfully in the potent Now with an unshakeable sense of personal empowerment. The potency of "Now" lies in its ability to serve as an elixir for the mind, offering relief from the burdens of dwelling on the past and worrying about the future. In the present moment, there is no room for the weighty and debilitating thoughts that often plague the mind. Instead, there is a sense of clarity, peace, and presence. By fully immersing yourself in the present moment, you can let go of regrets about the past and anxieties about the future, allowing for a profound sense of liberation and freedom. 'Now' serves as a powerful antidote to the stresses of life, offering a sanctuary of calm amidst the chaos of everyday existence, and true direction.

External circumstances will have less purchase on you as you commit to being 'true north' driven by the inner compass. This journey will allow you to access your full potential while staying true to your authentic self.

Remember, self-mastery is an ongoing adventure, not a quest for perfection or absolute control. It involves continuous self-reflection and personal growth, propelling you to new spiritual heights. **It is never about any sense of you having arrived!**

Embrace this journey with an open heart, and you'll uncover the extraordinary power within you to become all that you were meant to be. The path to selfrealization awaits – let your mindset be your guide, and you'll achieve greatness beyond imagination. Embedded within the vast expanse of cosmic consciousness lies a hyper-scalable Divine Intelligence – a force far mightier than your mind can fathom. Greatness in the context of self-realization is the attainment of one's highest potential and the realization of one's true nature. It spells the dissolution of the ego and recognises the interconnectedness of all beings. Greatness is not measured by external accomplishments or societal recognitions but by the depth of one's inner wisdom, compassion, and love. It is the ability to live in memberment with one's core values and principles while making positive contributions to life. Ultimately, greatness in self-realization is the journey towards spiritual awakening.

On your journey make **"I am Becoming"** your secret word or mantra. Gradually you will nurture a vast array of spiritual qualities. You will become instinctively aware of your thoughts, emotions, and actions.

Live with mindfulness and feel its enveloping presence spurring you to cherish each moment. Allow grace and humanity towards others to flow naturally from your heart. Let gratitude fill you, reminding you of life's blessings, while forgiveness liberates you from the burdens of the past. Your unique understanding of forgiveness and new insights and revelations will unearth a vital truth: the crucial battle preceding any external war lies within, where you must confront and overcome hatred and anger. With courage, extend a hand of friendship to your adversary, forging unity in both heart and mind. In winning this internal battle, you not only triumph in war but also in winning the world.

Any sense of abhorrence and any inclination to judge will recede as you humbly embrace acceptance and unadulterated purity. The yearning for unfolding will be your constant companion on this endless path to liberation.

As you live authentically and commune with the dense void of space within, a sense of inner peace will blossom. Trusting in the ebb and flow of life, you will find a strong connection with and the presence of the Divine in whatever way you perceive it - be it through religion, nature, or the Universe's grand design. Engaging in acts of service and altruism, you will see the beauty of Oneness, and each moment will offer a chance to push the barriers of limitation. Through this transformative journey, you will experience moments of awe and wonder, and your heart will swell with joy. With every step you take, you will evolve into the best version of yourself, radiating purpose and embracing life's magic.

The path to 'Becoming' has to be your purpose. Cherish each moment as you embrace the vastness that lies ahead.

In 'Becoming' your attributes are your protective sheath enabling you to ward off the clutches of hostile forces; slippery as mercury that you are.

11th Virtue

ON THE THRESHOLD
OF 'MUKTI'

Be in awe of the virtues you have acquired.
Speak ill of your goodness and the warring giant
within will die a small death.
Coax the treasure in you with empowering words and
the sleeping giant within will break all shackles!

As you step into the sacred realm of 'Mukti,' the chapter unfurls like an ancient scroll revealing the profound mysteries of liberation. The preceding wisdom has prepared you for this evolutionary pilgrimage, urging you to revere the virtues you symbolise and to exploit the power of uplifting words. Now, on the threshold of 'Mukti,' you stand at the precipice of spiritual liberation, beckoned by the call to self-realization. The quest for ultimate freedom – Mukti – begins with delving into the depths of your being and the heart of existence.

Mukti is a concept deeply rooted in some ancient spiritual traditions. It signifies the ultimate goal of human life; a state of eternal bliss and self-realization after emancipation from the cycles of suffering and the limitations of worldly existence. In its extreme, it may mean total liberation, freedom, or release from the cycle of birth, death, and rebirth where the individual soul reunites with the cosmic soul upon extinguishing the fires of all desire.

Contrary to common misperception, Mukti is not a sluggish state of doing nothing but rather a hyperactive state of enduring inner transformation of how life should be viewed and lived. Strange as it may appear, the entry into the state of Mukti begins with being worthy of and existing amid abundance consciousness so as not to care for accumulating possessions. It is understood when we are truly aware of the abundance that surrounds us, we no longer feel the need to hoard or accumulate material possessions. Instead, we recognize that we already have everything we need, and our focus shifts from acquiring more to appreciating and savouring what we already have. In this context, abundance can refer to anything from material wealth to personal relationships, good health, or spiritual fulfilment.

The abundance state as a prerequisite for Mukti leads to the gradual systematic cultivation of inner release and the understanding that a virtuous mind is synonymous with a virtuous being - that a virtuous mind serves as the bedrock for cultivating a virtuous being.

Central to the makeup of a virtuous being is the principle of **beneficence**, a character attribute that encompasses a range of benevolent actions and intentions. At its core, beneficence involves a genuine commitment to promoting the well-being of others. It goes beyond mere perfunctory acts of kindness and extends to a broader sense of moral obligation to contribute positively to the welfare of individuals, communities, and the broader world. A virtuous being, guided by beneficence, seeks opportunities to alleviate suffering, practise compassion, and enhance the overall quality of life for others.

The facets of beneficence are manifold, encompassing acts of charity, empathy, and selfless service. Whether through philanthropy, volunteering, or simply offering a compassionate ear, a virtuous being practices beneficence by actively contributing to the betterment of others. This principle also extends to the ethical use of one's skills, knowledge, and resources to uplift others, creating a ripple effect of nutritive wholesome impact.

Moreover, beneficence involves a deep sense of moral responsibility and a commitment to fairness and justice. It calls for advocating for the rights of the marginalized, standing against injustice, and actively working towards creating a more equitable and compassionate world.

Bob Geldof is an apt example of a being dedicated to fairness and justice. This Irish entertainer and philanthropist known for his tireless efforts to alleviate poverty and hunger in Africa gained international recognition in the 1980s for organizing charity concerts like Band Aid and Live Aid to raise funds for famine relief in Ethiopia. Geldof's commitment to humanitarian causes has continued over the years, as he has been involved in various initiatives advocating for debt relief for developing countries and promoting social justice.

In essence, beneficence, as the keystone of this virtuosity, embodies the understanding that true inner purity is not achieved in isolation but is intricately linked to the well-being and upliftment of others. It is through the practice of beneficence that the virtuous being, like Geldof, contributes to the co-creation of an idyllic existence for the collective human experience.

As you grasp the essence and wholeheartedly welcome beneficence into your being, the resonance of your mantra shifts from a personal journey of **"I am Becoming"** to a more expansive declaration of **"I am Becoming Beneficent."** This shift immerses you in the wider realm of beneficence, and your life ethos undergoes a profound expansion. You find enrichment in actions that transcend immediate gains, realizing that the true profit lies in selfless deeds – **profit from no profit deeds**. Beneficence becomes an integral part of your consciousness, evolving into your primary contribution to the world. You seamlessly align as a co-worker with Nature, and the sacred connection with the Maker is not only reaffirmed but strengthened - a spiritual umbilical cord binding you to the very source of existence.

You embody beneficence much like the majestic colossal blue whale. Even in its final moments of life, this magnificent creature performs an extraordinary leap out of the water, only to gracefully descend to its ultimate demise in the depths of the ocean. In this grand cycle of existence, the whale's decomposed remains become a vital source of nourishment for myriad tiny sea creatures and organisms, reinforcing the intricate web of marine life. As time unfolds, its colossal bones undergo a remarkable transformation, fossilizing into exquisite objects that bear witness to the awe-inspiring legacy of the benevolent giant.

Life unfolds harmoniously for you without the necessity of force, though diligent effort remains an inherent part of your journey. While some perceive life as a relentless toil, attributing success to luck, you recognize that even luck demands industrious endeavours. Yet, you pass through life with a graceful stride with equanimity, unburdened by conventional notions or dogmas. Others, amidst the vibrant mosaic of life's fluctuations, are drawn to your serene presence. Despite their independence to move swiftly, they seek the comfort of holding your hand, acknowledging your innate wisdom. This is the profound outcome of your manifestation of beneficence - a magnetism that transcends the mundane, making you a guiding light for those on the intricate pathways of existence and living life for its own sake.

As you stand on the threshold of Mukti, your journey of beneficence propels you forward into the realms of esoteric attributes yet to unfold. This chapter has been a gateway, revealing the transformative power of benevolence and compassion both sown within the Mukti state in which **you live as if you have nothing to lose, for all is yours.**

Now, armed with the understanding that beneficence is not just a singular attribute but a key that unlocks the gates to spiritual liberation, you step into the uncharted territories of Mukti. The path ahead holds the promise of unveiling deeper esoteric dimensions of beneficence, guiding you towards a more profound understanding of your spiritual potential.

One remarkable outcome derived from Mukti is spiritual liberation, culminating in the dissolution of various fears, particularly the fear of death, as profound esoteric insights become your ally. With this, you grasp life and eternity from the widest perspective. Consequently, you embark on living in a state of equanimity, allowing life to unfold serenely. You possess an intrinsic awareness of the time remaining in your life, enabling a calm surrender to the unfolding moments.

As you continue on this sacred journey, may the light of beneficence illuminate the path to Mukti, guiding you through the mysteries that lie ahead and opening your heart to the boundless possibilities of spiritual awakening.

12th Virtue

MASTERING MANIFESTATION

*Manifestation begins in earnest when beliefs and desires,
and dreams and fancies all become one and come dashing
at you like children set free after a hard day at school.*

Having embraced the foundational principles of Mukti and Beneficence, you are poised to step into the dynamic arena of conscious creation. Now, you will explore the intricate interplay between thought, energy, and reality, unlocking the latent power within you to consciously shape and manifest your desired outcomes. The journey extends beyond the ordinary into the extraordinary territory of manifesting intentions with heightened awareness. It's a co-creative process between the individual and the universal intelligence that governs existence.

You will unravel the secrets of conscious manifestation, an understanding that the ability to co-create with the Universe is not only a spiritual birthright but a potent force that, when harnessed with mindfulness, paves the way for a bountiful life filled with abundance, prosperity, and richness that goes beyond material wealth and encompasses abundance in relationships, health, opportunities, and personal growth overflowing with optimism and blessings. Such a life is characterized by gratitude, contentment, and an appreciation for the richness that nature has to offer. **What we appreciate appreciates.**

The seamless interweaving of thoughts, energy, and reality constitutes the foundation of this virtue. Manifestation is the process by which your thoughts and intentions are energetically transmitted to the responsive universe, aligning the external world with your internal desires in holistic connectedness.

Manifestation is the fulfilment of your manifesto.

It operates on the principle that the energy you emit attracts corresponding energies, shaping your reality. You must believe the universe is an inexhaustible hoard of all that a human mind can conceive. **The mind is not capable of conceiving anything that does not exist.** It cannot go beyond the universe, and that is its limit. To go into the uncharted realm beyond the universe, you have to shed your mind, or rather become mindless.

It is said, "To have sight but no vision is worse than being blind." Central to the manifestation process is the cultivation of a clear and compelling **Vision** - a vivid mental image of the outcomes you seek to bring into existence. It is the capacity or talent to see with clarity what is yet to materialize. Builders of great nations are, first of all, great visionaries. They envision their aspirations and desires in the chambers of their minds and are then inspired to take bold actions in the direction of their dreams.

Giving impetus to purpose, your vision serves as the vital compass guiding your goals and aspirations. As your senses inhabit this extraordinary territory, understanding the intricacies of manifestation and embracing the power of vision becomes not only a spiritual bequest but a conscious choice to co-create a reality that resonates with purpose, intention, abundance, and divine alignment. A compelling vision not only propels individuals forward but also galvanizes collective efforts toward a shared destiny. It is a blueprint for a certain transformation.

In the alchemy of conscious manifestation mastery, **Belief** emerges as another vital component, an ethereal thread weaving through the fabric of creation. Beliefs are seeds sown in the fertile territory of the subconscious mind. The subconscious mind will return what is planted in it, just like fertile land gives what is sown in it. Your beliefs function as the foundation stone of the bridge that connects the realm of thought to the materialization of your intentions. The power of manifestation is intricately tied to the strength and conviction of your beliefs. When you hold steadfast faith in the possibility of your envisioned outcomes, you amplify the resonance of your intentions within the energetic tapestry of the universe. Belief propels your thoughts from mere wishes to potent forces of transformation. As you delve into the extraordinary landscape of conscious manifestation, unwavering belief in the feasibility of your desires becomes the catalyst for this unimaginable transformation of your thoughts from mere wishes and deepest aspirations to sculpting your desired reality.

At the heart of conscious manifestation mastery lies the profound concept of **Aspiration** - an inner flame that ignites the journey towards the fulfilment of your deepest desires. Aspirations serve as guiding stars, directing the course of your intentions with clarity and purpose. When you align your intentions with genuine aspirations, you infuse them with a soulful energy that resonates with the core of your being, your silent chant. These aspirations act as powerful magnets, drawing universal energies into perfect alignment with your vision.

Vital in the entire gamut of manifestation, aspirations go beyond mere wishes; they encapsulate the essence of your truest self, reflecting your values, passions, and higher purpose. Nurturing aspirations instil a sense of purpose, fuelling the manifestation process with an unwavering dedication that propels your visions into tangible reality. As you sail the realms of conscious manifestation, acknowledging and refining your aspirations becomes the guide that keeps you true to your veritable path, ensuring that the outcomes you manifest are congruent with your soul's deepest yearnings.

A prudent note of caution accompanies the understanding that your aspirations mirror your deepest desires. It is crucial to differentiate these authentic aspirations from mere fantasies, which are akin to energy-less illusions conceived in a dormant mind. Sincerity in belief becomes paramount, acknowledging manifestation as an integral facet of pragmatic human endeavour. It's a force that never falters; however, attempting to test it without genuine conviction is bound to result in disillusionment. Manifestation thrives on serious intent and steadfast faith. Approach it with reverence, recognizing that your aspirations, grounded in sincerity, hold the transformative power to bridge the ethereal realm of thought with the tangible fabric of your lived experience.

This transformative power resides within you, waiting to be harnessed through intentional thought and purposeful action. Mastery in conscious manifestation requires a delicate orchestration of key elements: a vivid vision that serves as your guiding light, unwavering belief that fortifies the foundation of your intentions, sincere aspirations that resonate with the essence of your true self, and a profound understanding that manifestation is an integral aspect of pragmatic human endeavour. It necessitates a departure from mere fantasies, anchoring your manifestations in the realm of the possible.

Now add "I am Becoming a Manifester"
to your stable of mantras.

13th Virtue

EXPLORING THE ABSTRACT DESIGN BEHIND ALL LIFE

Where there is no science, mysticism thrives.
Do not delve into scholarly analysis. Embrace the experience.
Do not be paralyzed by the redness of the 'pink lady',
relish the taste of the apple.

One has to dare to go into the realm of the paranormal to become a consummate user of the mystical powers placed in all of us. Mystical powers entail a complex array of paranormal talents to **govern physical life**, spanning from the art of manifestation to the subtle nuances or tones of **healing, prophecy, soul travel, levitation, bi-location** and such siddhis which are different strands of one single thread of psychic realities. Psychic realities encompass mystical or transcendent experiences such as encounters with a higher consciousness or a sense of interconnectedness with the universe. Very simply, siddhis comprise piercing spiritual powers. **This segment of the Becoming phase is the pinnacle of the entire endeavour to cultivate a virtuous mindset.**

This unique journey serves as a metaphorical stethoscope,

allowing us to explore the depths of our inner selves and uncover latent potentials. It serves as a guide to reveal the hidden magic beyond our physical existence, urging us to boldly tap into the extraordinary abilities waiting to be discovered within us. While newcomers may initially feel overwhelmed by the wonders of their inner nature, engaging in the practice of mystical manifestation gradually transforms them into adept practitioners capable of achieving superhuman feats.

There are no miracles in life. Life itself is a miracle.
You and the universe are intertwined, composed of the
same cosmic particles, akin to mother and child.
Your expectations echo through the vast expanse of existence
and reverberate back in response to your innermost desires.

Perception, percolation, and performance form a natural cycle driven by our perceptions. We are inherently powerful beings, with our perceptions shaping the algorithms that guide our minds' reactions. These reactions, in turn, influence the inner chemistry of our bodies and our external environment. Immerse yourself in the liberating and self-empowering realm of mysticism, where the ordinary metamorphoses into the extraordinary, sometimes resembling the fantastical. These mystical abilities, often referred to as Siddhis among various terms, offer a glimpse into the realm of esoteric supernatural powers.

"**Siddhis**" is a term used in ancient yogic traditions, including the Yoga Sutras of Patanjali, to describe extraordinary, paranormal, or supernormal powers or abilities that are believed to be attainable through long periods of intense spiritual practice. These powers are not mere parlour tricks or magic, but manifestations of the vibrant consciousness and oneness with the universal energy that advanced practitioners attain. Siddhis are believed to be byproducts of the seeker's spiritual journey and are not pursued for personal gain or egoic reasons. They are a natural unfolding of spiritual evolution.

Moreover, these mystical powers are not deliberately sought after, other than in rare exceptional cases, but are considered by practitioners to be simply the fortuitous sprouting of advanced states of meditation and yoga.

Different types of siddhis encompass telepathy, clairvoyance, levitation, healing abilities, bi-location, telekinesis (the power to move objects), and control over the elements.

Learning these talents lacks a manual; they naturally emerge as blessings from the force of Creation. It's crucial to recognize that many traditions view siddhis as a potential distraction or even a black art, deviating from the true aim of spiritual enlightenment and self-realization. Practitioners primarily emphasize moral and ethical principles, self-discipline, and inner transformation. Any resulting siddhis, if they occur, are considered incidental and not intended for manipulation.

As the seeker advances on the path of 'Mukti' and the cultivation of 'Siddhi' powers, they become a conduit for '**Healing**', not only for themselves but also for others. Their heightened spiritual energy and connection to universal consciousness enable them to channel divine healing energies, bringing solace and relief to those in need. Additionally, the seeker becomes a '**Subliminal influencer**' of their environment, radiating positivity and compassion that subtly permeates the world around them, uplifting hearts and minds in profound ways.

One noticeable aspect that sets the seeker apart is the ethereal glow radiating from their being. This facial glow is not merely a physical phenomenon but a reflection of the inner transformation they have undergone. The seeker's face beams with serene tranquillity and a profound sense of peace, a testament to the inner harmony and spiritual wisdom they have attained. Their eyes sparkle with a profound knowing as if they have glimpsed the secrets of the universe. This radiant aura emanates from the depths of their soul, conveying their profound connection to the divine source of all existence. The seeker who has trawled beyond the domains visible to the naked eye sees no difference between life and death but only perpetuity.

The seeker's presence becomes a beacon of hope and inspiration, drawing others toward their spiritual light. Their mere presence has the power to soothe troubled souls, igniting a spark of divinity within those who come into contact with them. In the seeker's luminous countenance, one witnesses the embodiment of the groundbreaking journey they have undertaken - a journey that continues to unfold in wondrous ways as they walk the path of spiritual liberation and embrace the boundless potential of their awakened self.

In the formation of Siddhi powers, a remarkable realization unfolds - those who may not ascend to the pinnacle of such extraordinary abilities are nonetheless destined for an outcome of profound significance. This journey, while laden with the mystique of esoteric potentials, invariably bestows upon seekers an unparalleled gift: **extreme wisdom**. This is not merely the sagacity to decipher the mysteries of the universe but a profound understanding of human nature, compassion for oneself and others, and the ability to live with grace.

Much like the revered figures in history – Epictetus *(it is not the events that are terrible, but the interpretation we give them)*, Jidhu Krishnamurthi *(the real purpose of education......is to help us understand the whole process of life)* Thich Nhat Hanh *(....if one doesn't know how to die, one can hardly know how to live – because death is a part of life)* - whose wisdom transcended the ordinary, those on the plinth of Siddhi powers cultivate a depth of insight that permeates every facet of their existence. The bequest of Siddhi powers becomes a conduit for the acquisition of timeless wisdom, a treasure trove born from the fusion of experience, contemplations, and the unwavering pursuit of a virtuous mindset. They become a beacon of hope for all mankind.

And finally,

As we arrive after our shared odyssey through 'The Attributes of a Virtuous Mindset', my heart swells with gratitude for the journey we've embarked upon together. This work is not merely a compilation of ideas but a tapestry woven from the threads of my life experiences and learnings, spanning seven decades from my earliest childhood musings to the person I am now.

In each phase – 'Being,' 'Doing,' and 'Becoming' - we encountered the realms of awareness, intentional actions, and profound transformation. The understanding imparted within these pages is not just an intellectual exercise; it is a heartfelt offering, a sincere desire to share the profound wisdom and insights gleaned from the collective teachings of revered thinkers.

Wisdom and insights play significant roles in personal growth, understanding, and decision-making. They serve as catalysts for growth and transformation.

Wisdom is a deep understanding of life, people, and situations, gained from influences, experiences, reflection, and learnings with the application of emotional intelligence, knowledge and judgment to contend with complex situations and make sound decisions. Wisdom also encompasses empathy and ethical considerations.

Insights, contrastingly, are like sudden bursts of clarity that spontaneously illuminate the mind, offering new understanding or fresh perspectives. These revelations occur when the mind is open and receptive. In their interconnectedness, wisdom and insights symbiotically nourish and enhance each other. Wisdom serves as the bedrock upon which insights (those "Eureka moments") emerge, broadening perspectives and enriching understanding.

As you reach the conclusion of this final chapter, may the essence of our exploration stay with you - a virtuous mindset rooted in purpose, intention, and alignment with the divine. Let your aspirations shine like guiding stars, leading you towards a life of bliss that reflects the authenticity of your true self.

Yet, do not be deceived into thinking you've reached the end of your journey; you are merely on the threshold of self-realisation. However, it's essential to acknowledge a caveat: **there is no ultimate destination when your consciousness expands into uncharted territories.** In this expansion, you may encounter unbounded nothingness, the potential source of all manifestation, the ending of search!

> A deep-seated feeling that after all you've done,
> you have still not arrived, and the
> worthlessness of it all, is the beginning of
> self-realisation, a leap from real to reality.

As we reach the culmination of this transformative journey, may the currents of your enlightened mind ripple outward, lifting not only your own vessel but also those of others around you. Let the beacon of your innate goodness and greatness illuminate the path for others, inspiring upliftment and growth in every heart and soul you touch.

With heartfelt gratitude,

Thank you.

Anil

My Working Creed

This is my statement of beliefs that I seek to hold as my constant companion.

I believe my thoughts are the trigger to all that I experience, and how I interpret what I experience determines my form.

I am the result of my thoughts. Everything in my reciprocating world begins with a thought, and so for peace in my life, I endeavour hard to abstain from thoughts of harm toward others. The more I practise this abstention and the more I reach out to others, the more I reap incalculable returns when I least expect them.

When stymied at life's crossroads, I believe that to seek the path that aligns me with the purpose of the Higher Force will create harmony at the deepest level, and lead me to my destiny. The true purpose of the Higher Force is to inspire and give certitude, a feeling of absolute certainty necessary in nurturing my creative talents.

Therefore, when I inspire others, I believe I am letting the Higher Force act through me as its instrument. To strive not to take credit for any such deeds, and to put the glory of such deeds in the lap of the Higher Force is an act of supreme humility.

I believe that my truest sense of liberation from the shackles of social conditioning will come when I am free of judgment, and when I accept everything without condemnation.

I believe that only when I am free of judgment and prejudice, only when race, religion, gender, status, titles, accumulations and all descriptions become secondary to my true purpose in life, will I begin to experience the Divine and manifest my destiny.

I believe that there are no bad or evil human beings, only prisoners of warped thinking, reflecting aspects in me that may now be extinct. These distinctions will cease to be when these fellow beings board my bus of life journey into the infinite inner world.

I believe that to strive to amass wealth is not immoral, but it is a form of lust when it ceases to be a goal and becomes a purpose, a perpetual grind, in life. Accumulated wealth is a myth; until it is put to use for the general and common good, it is not true wealth, only a burdensome yoke.

I believe that man does not need religion to experience God, and the real truth is that which I have uncovered for myself, and not that which is thrust upon me. The higher truth, though, is that there is no real point in holding vehemently on to such truths, for yesterday's truth is today not what it was, and tomorrow will bring another superseding truth.

I strive to remain open-minded and let the mysteries of life continue to bewilder me.

I believe that to see a good hidden purpose or joy and glory in all events of existence and in every circumstance is the truest form of expression of gratitude. Behind every event, the supreme intelligent Force has a purposeful hand, and to credit it with all that happens in my world is the beginning of true emancipation – the beginning of the need not to possess anything, or be anyone other than my true self.

-Anil Kumar

Printed in the United States
by Baker & Taylor Publisher Services